"*Journey to Light is vast in scope, deep in insight, saturated with wisdom, and expressed with bright beauty. I am certain that it will touch many lives.*"

- Francis Rico
  Author of "A Shaman's Guide to Deep Beauty"

"*Journey to Light is a very valuable contribution to the Recovery literature. The basis for the narrative, the mythological struggle between the Eagle and the Condor, represents the ongoing human process to find a balance in which individuals and communities can live and blossom. The principles illustrated by the author to facilitate the path to Recovery provide a valuable guide on how to reach a state of individual and community awareness in which Recovery transcends the boundaries of individual problems with substances, and assumes the deeper meaning of a restoration of balance for individuals, communities, and the entire planet. Moreover, the work is not a theoretical narrative, but offers a very pragmatic approach on how to foster, attain, and disseminate the essence of recovery*".

- Dr. Marcello A. Maviglia, MD, MPH
  Associate Professor, UNM/ Department of Family And Community Medicine/ Institute For Indigenous Knowledge And Development, Albuquerque, NM

Journey to Light

The Eagle Condor Principles

Serving Humanity's Recovery

by

Gordon Eagleheart

Original eagle image created by Crystal McEwan Photography

Original Eagleheart Logo created by Elizabeth Derecktor, Spiritwear

Other Artwork and Graphics by Gordon Eagleheart

ISBN-13:
978-1522771623

ISBN-10:
152277162X

Library of Congress Control Number (LCCN): 2015921243

CreateSpace Independent Publishing Platform,
North Charleston, SC

www.gordoneagleheart.com

www.journeytolight.info

To order more copies of this book, please visit:

https://www.createspace.com/5941085

Acknowledgements

Everyone I have encountered on my journey through life was a valuable contributor to the creation of this book. I cannot mention one without omitting a precious beloved. Thus I choose not to name individual people.

I thank all those who shared difficulties with me. I'm grateful for all your open hearts as we nurtured each other through challenging times.

I wish to acknowledge my greatest teachers; The Sandia Mountain, The Desert Mesa and the Rio Grande Bosque in New Mexico. They taught me how to commune with our Mother Earth. And special thanks to the magnificent pine tree in Embudito Canyon. Your patience and acceptance helped me find clarity and supported me.

I acknowledge you, the reader. Thank you for being here at this time of great transition. You are a vital link in the web of Life. What you do does make a difference.

"Out of the Indian approach to life there came a great freedom, an intense and absorbing respect for life, enriching faith in a Supreme Power, and principles of truth, honesty, generosity, equity, and brotherhood as a guide to mundane relations."

- Black Elk
Oglala Lakota (1863-1950)

CONTENTS

CHAPTER FIVE

CHAPTER SIX

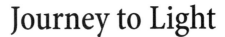

Journey to Light

The Eagle Condor Principles

Serving Humanity's Recovery

CHAPTER ONE

A Plea

There is a cry, a plea, an asking echoing in canyons, bouncing off river banks and humming everywhere. This appeal resonates in all trees, birds, animals and fish. It's a song floating universally in sweet lovely harmony. It's in the wind, water, earth and all the fires of the universe. Flowers sing it. Foods in grocery stores hum it. Dogs bark to it while cats purr along. A grand glorious chorus is singing a delightful calling and it is here every day and every night.

The cry is in the leaves as they flutter in the breeze. The plea is in the air that blows through the trees. Water dances; keeping a beat, whistling with the chorus. Cranes sing along; crying in collaboration. Monkeys swing in rhythm from tree to tree. Dragonflies buzz to it. Horses prance to it. Flowers bloom in it. Trees sing, praying it is heard. Life, in all its grandeur, sings an inviting song.

The breeze whispers sharing Life's desire, "Do you hear us, Giant?"

Hope is caressed by lovely yearning and bathed in unconditional love. Life sings with passion, seeking harmonic unity. The melody whirrs in clouds, dances on ocean waves and resonates everywhere. Seasons transition and the song goes on with longing lingering.

"Please, Giant, hear us and sing along!"

The song of Life rings though water and air; echoing through trees. Fires of Life fuel the hymn as Earth embraces all. The grand chorus sings, pursuing harmony with every voice. Connection through interwoven consciousness guides the music's flow. Voices go silent as species decline. The desire for harmony demands death to adjust voices for synchronized melody. Longing lingers as chords resonate through Life. Will the Giant hear the inviting song?

The Giant sleeps alone; dreaming a dream. The ground trembles as the Giant tosses and turns. The Giant's dream is consuming; fueled by fear. The Giant shouts while asleep; demanding and commanding. The Giant's voice shakes everything. It's thunderous and domineering! The Giant hears no chorus. The Giant feels no melody, no harmony. The Giant is lost in a dream that controls and seeks ever more!

What will it take to awaken the Giant and allow the Giant's voice to join the chorus of Life?

If the Giant remains asleep, what will become of Life's choir?

It's time to turn the page.

Introduction

Our world is composed of many worlds in the same way our body is composed of many cells that come together to form the vessel we live in. We have a personal world, family world, social world and natural world. All these worlds combine to form the wonderful world we call planet Earth. Life's song sings through all these worlds. The song resonates and vibrates in matter and harmonizes with thoughts and emotions. A great song is being sung that serves to nurture and support the continuity of Life. This book exists to help humanity awaken, learn to listen and join the chorus of Life.

The condition of the Earth and the condition of our society are showing signs of dysfunction and unsustainability. The signs are saying we need to acknowledge that our behaviors are causing harm to ourself and others. This is the same message that is delivered to anyone who suffers with addiction. Our culture is filled with growing addictions. They are on display in personal lives and in social systems. Humanity's addictions are causing harm to all Life.

Those who choose to live a life in recovery are the seeds of growth in human consciousness. They may not know it, but they are forging a new frontier. As people change, they change the world. People living in recovery are learning the skills we all need to learn if we are to shift from unhealthy dysfunctional patterns to lifestyles that are sustainable and healthy. This book is meant to nurture a recovery movement in humanity. The principles presented are designed to support the awakening process to heal and unify us. All of humanity is suffering from our disharmonious ways. We are the Giant who is asleep dreaming a dream that prevents us from living in harmony with ourself, each other and all of Nature.

In the Andes of South America and areas of Central America a prophecy is told of a cycle between the Eagle and Condor. Eagle represents the mind, rational, materialism and masculinity. Condor represents the heart, intuition, generosity and femininity. During the cycles of time the two exchange dominance in the sky. At one time Condor flew alone in the sky. Consciousness was ruled by the heart, intuition and feeling. The sacred feminine was honored and generosity was abundant. Then Eagle rose and drove Condor from the sky. The rational mind, materialism and need to control gained dominion of consciousness. It's no accident that the Roman standard prominently displayed an eagle. To this day, Eagle remains a symbol of power and strength. Eagle has driven Condor from our sky. We are coming to the end of the cycle of Eagle. We are entering a time of great transition. It's time to welcome Condor's return to our sky.

We are entering a new age, a time when Eagle and Condor will fly together sharing the sky. For us to recover and heal we need to develop balance between mind and heart, rational and intuitive, masculine and feminine, competition and collaboration, the individual and collective. The principles presented in this book provide guidance for conscious communion. When applied in our lives, these principles manifest harmony between consciousness and our sacred self.

The essence of our existence communes with the song of Life through spirit, body and mind. Health arrives when the three are in harmony. Those working to restore balance are walking a path of recovery. All are striving to unify and heal. We are all seeking, unity, purity, health and well-being. This book echoes a calling from Life to stir the desire within humanity to awaken and dream a new dream; a healthy dream that serves the continuity of Life. This book exists to serve the recovery of humanity; to return us to our true divine nature.

A Taste of My Journey

On a soggy, sunless, grey afternoon a profound experience shook the foundation of my reality and changed my universe. I was in a dark state of mind where no light shines. I saw futility everywhere. My life was unacceptable. Life wasn't worth living. I felt no hope. No desire to continue. Existence served no purpose. Irrational thoughts were rational. Emotionless numbness comforted me as my mind ran marathons seeking answers. Feeling nothing allowed me to focus on my perpetual stream of thoughts.

My mind was stuck in an irreconcilable loop of logic constantly asking the question, *How can I tell if it's God's intention or my destiny to kill myself?* My mind wanted to know if I was supposed to commit suicide. I was frustrated because no amount of logical reasoning could create a clear conclusion. At times the answer seemed to be death but a doubt remained, *What if it's true that if we take our own life, we must suffer the same things over and over until we learn to live through those difficulties?* This inquiry prevented me from committing the final act. I was trapped in hell. I loathed this life. I didn't want to live and I certainly didn't want to repeat this life again. I cursed all that was! I hated being alive; trapped in this life!

I gazed upon a misty courtyard through the window of my mental health hospital room. The dreary overcast sky perfectly matched my feelings. Darkness was in everything at midafternoon. No trees moved, no leaves turned, not a single bird sang or flew as I stared into a motionless natural world. Each breath was a struggle. Deep in hopelessness I mumbled, "How can I know my destiny?"

The yard began to alter as the last sounds passed my lips. Glimmering silver embers appeared on the grass and tree leaves. A bird flew by leaving a shiny trail of translucent waves.

The clouds started shimmering. A new sensation emerged. Goosebumps brought the hair on my arms to attention. Then the clouds, trees, shrubs, leaves, grass and sidewalk began vibrating. Everything moved while remaining still. A glowing sheen floated off the clouds above and all in the courtyard below. The spirit of Life emerged like a ghost rising from a body. I was mesmerized; awestruck, as the specter coiled itself into a tubular worm-shape. Then in a flash it struck! Like a snake striking; the apparition struck across the courtyard, through the window and entered my chest. The blow knocked me back several feet.

My chest expanded as sensations of wholeness, connection, satisfaction, joy and bliss consumed me. I experienced being part of universal consciousness that is everywhere and in everything. I clearly felt the answer I desperately sought. I quickly scrambled for a notepad and pen and wrote; *Look into your heart. What does it say? What is the answer to the question? Who decides when it is time for life to depart? The answer is NOT ME! It's not my job to determine when I depart this life. It never has been, never will be. My job is to live! Thru good, thru bad! All there is to do is live.*

I placed the notepad down and noticed the green color pencil in my hand looked very strange. I had never seen anything like it. It was glowing and didn't have solid edges. I felt aliveness in the wood; like a humming electric motor. I looked at my room and everything glowed and vibrated while remaining stationary. I felt aliveness in the chair, bed, covers, and pillow. I could feel everything smiling and holding me in a loving embrace. A new world appeared and it was an amazing place of interwoven connectedness; where feelings and thoughts are shared. Everything is a blending and merging of intent in an endless flowing river of Life. Energy dances with matter. And matter reflects Life energy. Everything is alive. Everything feels. We are a part of something amazingly grand and conscious. The gigantic web of Life was revealed and experienced by me for approximately 20 minutes.

I was blessed with a gift as the experience faded. As my ability to feel the aliveness of matter dissolved, I saw what was separating me from divine communion; my mind was coming back on line. The more I thought about what I was experiencing; the greater the speed of departure. Eventually I returned to how I had been most of my life. Only now, something was radically different. I had been given a taste of honey. I smelled roses for the first time. Within me resided a certainty that can only arrive with experience. I possessed a realization like the flavor of strawberries. I discovered that another form of consciousness exists; one I never imagined possible. And it is a magnificent place. I also knew that my thinking was preventing me from experiencing this other dimension.

A burning desire to learn how to return to such a state of communion was lit in me and with it an unquenchable thirst for more of that grand experience of Life. I was determined to nurture this flame and learn how to be alive in every moment. My journey to light began that fateful afternoon at Midcoast Hospital in Brunswick, Maine on September 14, 2006.

I shared my exciting awakening experience with the clinical staff at the hospital. My doctor said, "I'm glad the medicine is kicking in." As I shared my intense discoveries of another way to perceive the universe and how everything is alive, I witnessed eyes roll-over or become glazed. I was excited to be alive and felt reborn. I was given a chance to create a new life. The staff was pleased I was no longer suicidal and managed to create a diagnosis from my expressions.

I quickly learned that what I experienced could not be comprehended by the medical professionals in charge of my health. And being a scientist with advanced degrees in engineering limited my ability to understand the profound spiritual aspects of my encounter with universal consciousness. At first I accepted the story provided by the medical professionals; drugs had caused me to have a psychotic episode that manifested delusions that seemed real. However, no scientific reasoning could explain the state of "certainty" that remained. The realism within me was beyond doubt. I saw that my beliefs and the explanations provided by others were not supporting my return to the dimension of universal oneness and divine communion with Life. I needed to find other sources of wisdom.

I researched, studied and practiced numerous spiritual and medical techniques for recovery. I left my engineering and business life and entered the behavioral health world. I developed an understanding of human interaction and dysfunctional behavior while working as a substance abuse counselor and peer support specialist. My knowledge and skills increased along with an ability to commune with a grander consciousness. I felt a calling. It was an insatiable sensation; like what a salmon must feel when it's time to swim upstream. I followed and the summons guided me to Albuquerque, New Mexico.

Unexpectedly, my credentials were not accepted in my new homeland. My few remaining plans crumbled. I felt destiny say, *You're here to learn the way of spirit and shamanism. Leave the ways of modern education. Let them be road signs of a highway you once traveled.* I developed relationships and learned with Lakota and Dine' elders and practiced with Toltec, Aztec and Mayan shaman. I acquired skills to obtain altered states of consciousness without the use of substances. I learned how to return to that place others called a delusion. I discovered that shamanic altered states access wisdom that has guided humanity for eons.

A calling came for a vision quest in the Sandia Mountains. It arrived through drum journeying and dream work. Again I followed the calling. I returned to the state of conscious communion with Life while fasting and tending sacred fire within a medicine wheel. Hummingbirds watched over me. They visited three times each day - sunrise, noontime and sunset. A peregrine falcon told me it was time to rise above my situation and seek a higher vision. I listened to the summon and journeyed higher up the mountain. Each step was an effort as I learned how to receive assistance from stones, shrub oaks, grasses and even cacti. Everything was shimmering and vibrating. As I reached the peak, I saw an eagle, or was it a condor, soaring just above a tree top. Then another appeared and circled round and departed to the west. Another arose from the east, circled and left, then another. I counted five. I felt a rush of energy, like an electric shock, pulse through my body. Wisdom echoed through my body. After many tears of gratitude, I hiked back to my medicine wheel and completed my cry for a vision.

The vision I received charged me with a task to deliver a message to my human family to help them through these times of great transition. The five eagles or condors represent five principles for recovery. They are an offering to humanity to help us learn how to break free of our dysfunctional patterns of behavior and create a new human dream. The principles serve to harmonize our mind and heart and balance our consciousness with Life.

Science will collaborate with spirituality; brothers will embrace sisters; modern thought will respect indigenous wisdom; the teachings of all the religions will unite to honor purity; and Love will comfort Fear as we recover balance and harmony with ourselves, each other and Nature. The time has come for humanity to become one family and nurture and support each other. The time has come for war to end and peace on Earth to manifest.

"*The first peace, which is the most important, is that which comes within the souls of people when they realize their relationship, their oneness, with the universe and all its powers, and when they realize that at the center of the universe dwells Wakan-Taka (the Great Spirit), and that this center is really everywhere, it is within each of us.*

This is the real peace, and the others are but reflections of this. The second peace is that which is made between two individuals, and the third is that which is made between two nations. But above all you should understand that there can never be peace between nations until there is known that true peace, which, as I have often said, is within the souls of men."

- Black Elk - Oglala Lakota (1863-1950)

Our Journey Begins

The intent of this book is to guide you, the reader, on a voyage of discovery. The text can be thought of as signposts pointing to places to explore. The adventure is a personal journey filled with wonder and amazing discoveries to help you master the essence of your individuality. Many ideas and relationships will be described. You are encouraged to embrace what you read as an opportunity to explore what makes sense to you. As you read, ask yourself if this fits with your experiences in life. If you feel the resonance of common sense being stimulated, this book is for you. Go deeper, explore and participate. Amazing freedom and bliss will manifest in your life.

Basic principles of how consciousness interacts with life force energy and our thoughts and emotions will be presented. I have chosen words as best I can to describe my observations during my journey from extreme discontent and great emotional suffering to true joy in living. I invite the reader to pretend you are at a clothing store trying on clothes. Treat the concepts and relationships presented as articles of clothing. Try them on and see how well you look. The value of this book resides between the words and lingers in you, the reader. There is magic here and if you feel it and summon it, you will discover a new world.

There are numerous ideas and terms we will be using as we explore The Eagle Condor Principles. Let's create some common meaning as we prepare to depart on a journey to light and authentic living.

<u>What is a principle?</u>

A principle is a law or rule that describes inevitable consequences when followed or not followed. Here are some natural principles we can observe: Water flows downhill. Objects fall down, not up. Hot things cool, thus heat flows from hot to cold. When we open a door to a dark room, light goes into the dark room rather than darkness entering the lit room, thus, light flows into darkness. We discover fundamental governing principles through observation.

Our society is beginning to see how our failure to respect underlying natural principles is affecting life on our planet. Climate change, species extinction, social inequality and spiritual decay are consequences from our failure to follow deep-seated natural laws. The same is true regarding the forces of recovery. Failing to respect basic principles maintains the status quo and keeps us imprisoned in emotional suffering and discontent. Unwanted habitual ways continue until we obey important rules. Natural laws are guides for harmonious existence.

Learning fundamental principles and practicing them is how we live life in recovery. When we do so, a shift in our experience happens. We learn how to manifest peace and harmony rather than unhappiness and discord. We realize our power to create. Unhealthy destructive patterns of behavior become healthy, supportive actions. Our heart and mind sing in harmony. We become the stewards of our experience by applying basic rules. We master how we create emotions, sensations and feelings. Through practice, we stop creating emotional suffering and disharmony. Our use of principles is how we change our world.

What is recovery?

I chose the word recovery because it is a commonly used term for people seeking to change undesired patterns in life. The details and specific meaning of recovery vary from person to person but common themes exist. The phrase, "living in recovery" means we're living a lifestyle free from old patterns that no longer work. We restore our true nature and our authentic presence shines bright. We return to being true to who we really are. We hear our genuine calling and live as we're meant to live.

SAMHSA (Substance Abuse and Mental Health Services Administration) defines Recovery from Mental Disorders and Substance Use Disorders as follows: "A process of change through which individuals improve their health and wellness, live a self-directed life, and strive to reach their full potential." This applies to every human I have encountered, with or without a diagnosis. Recovery is for everyone.

Recovery is a word that speaks of creating a new life from an old one. Living in recovery is mastering the way of the Phoenix. The Phoenix is a sacred firebird found in many mythologies. The Phoenix represents a cycle. First the bird builds a comfortable nest. Then the Phoenix hears the calling for change. It willingly burns in flames so it may be reborn. The Phoenix embraces its own end in order to bring forth a new beginning. The poem below was found in ancient Roman ruins.

The bird proudly willing to burn,
So that he may live again,
Chooses the flames of fires
That burn the aged Phoenix
The nature stands still
Till a new young bird starts again
And begins the legend of the Phoenix
    - Claudian (Roman author)

The Phoenix story describes the spirit of recovery. It is a symbol of transformation. What is required for all who are successful in recovery is a proud willingness to burn in order for a new way of living to emerge. This means a readiness to let go of old habits to make way for new actions. The aged must burn to prepare the nest for the new. As we learn how our old habits limit us, we let them go so we can begin practicing ways that nurture and support a healthy lifestyle.

Are you willing to look inside and seek old nests that require burning? Is there a willingness in you to burn the old and make room for new beginnings? New life will not emerge until space is created for fresh growth. A willingness to create space often requires the destruction of old, familiar, unhealthy patterns that, in a strange way, have been providing both comfort and dissatisfaction. Clearing away the old to make way for the new is the process of recovery.

The Recovery Process

Recovery is change. We can either resist or accept the process. Those who succeed in recovery and move the fastest are the ones who embrace change and master basic aspects. The three fundamental elements of the recovery process are: Awareness, Transformation and Intent.

Awareness

Whenever we're stuck in a rut of dysfunctional behavior, we are unaware of our entire situation. We're blind to different perspectives. Other ways to look at our condition are not possible. For example, an alcoholic doesn't see how drinking is impacting their life or the life of others around them. They often think drinking is a good thing. It's supporting them by helping relieve the stress of life. They're unable to see that other perspectives are valuable. Awareness opens the door to possibilities that are not otherwise seen. Mastering awareness is a critical aspect to develop and will be explored on this journey.

Transformation

Once we become aware that a problem exists, we begin to take action to correct it. Transformation is change occurring through action. Old habitual ways are identified with awareness. Then new ways of being with the situation are created during the transformative facet of recovery. Once a heavy drinker becomes aware that their condition is not serving them, they take actions that support change. For example; drinking to relieve stress is replaced with meditation, supportive conversations, or physical exercise. This shift in action is the transformation aspect of recovery. All life is engaged in transformation; it's called growth. During this adventure we'll see that change is a natural part of life.

Intent

If we think of living in recovery as driving a car: awareness is paying attention to where we are going, the speed limit and the conditions of the road. Transformation is steering the car, applying pressure on the pedals and all the actions required to drive the car. Intent is the gas that runs the engine. Intent is the fuel that sustains our journey.

Intent is the force that keeps things going and to understand it, we examine energy interactions. Energy is used to pay attention and observe our condition. Awareness requires energy. It also takes energy to change and do things differently. Thus, transformation also uses energy. Where does the energy come from? The force that keeps the cycle moving is intent. When people burn out and give up, it is because they have lost the intent to continue. They haven't learned how to manage the flow of life force energy in a way that sustains, nurtures and promotes continued growth. They haven't mastered intent.

All three aspects of the recovery cycle are important. I call them the recovery masteries. They are the core skills to be mastered on your journey to light. The figure below is a handy reference diagram that shows the key elements and the flow of the cycle of recovery.

THE RECOVERY PROCESS

MASTERY OF AWARENESS

See, Look, Discover

Identify
Unexamined
Assumptions

MASTERY OF TRANSFORMATION

Act, Do, Change

Stop dysfunctional habits
Create healthy patterns

MASTERY OF INTENT

Maintain Motivation
Nurture Faith
Empowerment

The recovery process is a cycle of change. It's a natural growth cycle. Tiny caterpillars use awareness to find delicious leaves to consume. They grow until they hear the call for transformation. They toil creating a cocoon. Within their creation they transform. Then they struggle with strong intent out of their confinement. With new wings the intent to lay eggs and nurture new growth emerges. They fly off using awareness to find a mate and procreate.

Like all of nature's creations, we use awareness to learn and discover. Awareness is our ability to see what does and doesn't support our growth. It helps us examine how we look at things; allowing us to identify the unexamined assumptions that limit us and sustain our suffering. Insights offer opportunity to break-up dysfunctional habits and replace them with healthy patterns. The actions we take toward change are transformational. In order to maintain our motivation, we learn how to nurture our faith to continue. Learning how to empower ourself and others is mastering the power of intent. It keeps the light of recovery burning.

<u>Why Eagle Condor Principles?</u>

We live in challenging times. Modern society is being forced to realize that what we do to others we do to ourselves. Climate change, species extinction and numerous other trends are guiding us to awaken. The phrase, "wake up" is becoming common. As a collective, people are increasing their awareness, many are calling for transformation of our political and social systems. We're realizing that we're connected and not separate. Great change is happening on this planet. The same is occurring in each of us. We are transforming and evolving.

Look how things have changed. During The Renaissance, scientists like Copernicus and Galileo were considered heretics by church leaders. Science and religion were in opposition. The Catholic Church gave permission for countries to "colonize" indigenous people's land. Now we live in a time of great turning. Systems of power suppress scientific knowledge, while the leader of the Catholic Church sides with science and indigenous people. Pope Francis wrote of our relationship with Earth, "We have grown up thinking that we were her owners and dominators, authorized to loot her. The violence that exists in the human heart, wounded by sin, is also manifest in the symptoms of illness that we see in the Earth, the water, the air and in living things."[1] This is very significant. As a collective, we are being asked by universal consciousness to acknowledge the relatedness and sacredness of all things.

The medical approach to recovery is moving with this great shift. Within the behavioral health community there's a growing acceptance that spirituality has value in recovery. There's budding desire to find ways to bring the medical and spiritual approach together. Meditation, yoga and a variety of religious ceremonies and practices are being recognized as valuable for health.

There is a lack of clarity concerning how to speak about the divine component of life. Twelve step programs use God and higher power to introduce spirituality. Medical professionals use disease to describe human conditions and limit participation in the sacred aspects. Both groups need ways to bridge the gap between spiritual and medical health practice. This book targets those seeking to move forward across this canyon.

The holistic approach to health advocates balance among Spirit, Body and Mind. Each is an equal participant with equivalent importance. Each serves and nurtures the other two. They are inseparable. When harmony exists between them, health manifests. When we have discord we experience disease. This it true for every individual. It's also true of the collective.

The Eagle Condor Principles are laws of nature that govern consciousness. They are presented in a language of recovery so the reader can embrace the natural rules that guide us to harmony between mind and the sacredness of Life. Eagle represents the mind. Condor represents spirit. And the body is the expression of their communion in material form.

When the mind dominates; creating spiritual suppression, we manifest disease, emotional suffering and devastation. The modern industrial world's dysfunction comes from our lack of harmony with the spiritual. Climate chaos, environmental degradation and social injustice are all signs of this imbalance.

When spirit dominates; producing mind suppression, we journey into la-la land with little physical expression. Life wants us to sing, dance, play music and create spectacular harmonious splendor. We are here to be balanced, not biased.

Modern society is out of balance. And since everything is related, we are out of balance. Jiddu Krishnamurti put it well, "It is no measure of health to be well adjusted to a profoundly sick society."[2] We can recover from our illness. We need a recovery movement that applies basic principles to humanity's collective consciousness to heal our society. We mend one person at a time. It's important to know that what you do for yourself, you are doing for all life.

It's time for the eagle and condor to fly together. It's time to allow the mind and heart to unite and touch the wisdom within. We're being asked by universal consciousness to become whole and complete; to let go of illusions that prevent us from being our authentic harmonious self. The nights of competition, self-centeredness and greed are ending. The days of collaboration, altruism and generosity are rising.

The way we change the world is by changing ourselves.

CHAPTER TWO

The Lullaby of Knowledge

*"The first people had questions and they were free.
The second people found answers and were imprisoned."*

-Ancient Wisdom

Each of us arrives in a state of inquisitive curious wonder. We're empty vessels innocent with no knowledge. Within us is a drive to explore and discover. Watch any baby and observe an amazing life force within a fresh human body. The baby touches everything it can and seeks to feel as many sensations as possible. Tiny hands grasp as the human seedling learns how fingers operate. Everything is brought to the mouth so the tastes of this new world can be explored. Children show us our true nature. We're here to observe, discover and experience the wonders of being human.

Most babies grow and discover how to use both knees and hands. Crawling and movement are explored and the world expands beyond the blankets, carriers and cribs. Toddlers continue their adventure, discovering more as senses become stronger with use. *This tastes wonderful, that's not too good. Embraces soothe. Loud sounds are scary. Hunger hurts and eating satisfies.* Familiarity of many relationships manifest as the young mind records discoveries, creating memories and attachments.

Children develop strong relatedness with their body by the time they reach the age of two. Their mind has much to learn. They're both playful and serious. The imagined and "real" worlds have equal influence. Living in the moment dominates their life. And consequences of actions are difficult to comprehend. They're wild and free humans. We call this period of growth, "the terrible twos", because language and social etiquette haven't been mastered and exploration is overwhelmingly exciting! They're wild mustangs, unbroken, without knowledge to hold the reins of their mind. They have yet to be domesticated. Gradually shared meanings and correctness are learned. Natural curiosity continues as rules and roles are absorbed.

When I was very young, I was innocent, ignorant and inquisitive. Exploration was life. Imagination was my way of living. Most mornings I awoke with anticipation, longing to pretend something exciting and grand. My friends and I played, pretending fantastic adventures. We travelled to other worlds and past times. We shared dreams and overcame great adversity. Our cooperation and collaboration created amazing escapades. The capers were rich and full of excitement. We were alive in every imagined moment. Time stopped. Then we'd hear the call for dinner or bedtime. We'd leave our dream world wishing our playtime would never end.

I played with my friends for years. All the while, something was growing in each of us. We had no awareness of its existence. We only noticed the effects. Friends stopped wanting to pretend. Imagining other worlds and fantasizing adventures lost their appeal. Girls became interesting and pretending to be pirates or baseball stars seemed childish. Our focus shifted to real sports and real activities. Pretend was for kids. Now was the time to be adults. Life became serious. We learned the rules and roles of important play. Our knowledge of how to be in the world grew as our minds and bodies developed.

My knowledge became my friend, my guardian. It helped me understand how the world works. I discovered the worst thing to say in school is, "I don't know." Teachers wanted some answer. Saying you don't know meant you're lazy or not trying. It was better to make something up and guess than to admit you don't know. Teachers preferred to correct me. They liked that I was participating. Life in school was about having the right answer or knowing how to find it. With correct answers I got better scores, good grades and more acceptance and praise. I learned that there's great value in having answers and being right.

Unfortunately, I never figured out how to get the right answers for girls, or how to deal with emotional turmoil that causes pain. That is until I found the magic of alcohol and drugs. They were my answer, my escape from fear of rejection and the pain of non-acceptance. The world loved me when I was high. Substances helped me hide from what I didn't want to feel. And I obtained more knowledge through their use. I learned how to avoid emotions I didn't like. I was able to feel my free childish ways by using intoxicating substances. I felt embraced and loved while high. But the effects wore off and required more each time I used.

This is how my problems started. My journey through darkness began when I accepted my knowledge as truth. My explanations for why I felt anger, jealousy, envy, resentment and self pity all made perfect sense. I had sound reasons for using substances. All my answers for how things work were telling me that I'm doing what's "right". It never dawned on me that I could be mistaken, that my knowledge was inaccurate and controlling me. I was living without awareness. I was in the dark; struggling through unhappiness, seeking to escape emotional pain. I had become imprisoned by the answers I had found.

We come into this world alert and awake, without knowledge. Curiosity and exploration is our natural state. Answers about the unknown provide security. A sense of knowing consoles us as we drift into cozy sleep. Our knowledge comforts us like a warm blanket or bedtime story; our knowledge reassures us.

We hear the lullaby of "sleep baby sleep" as we accept our training. Our awake, alert and curious explorer listens to knowledge and falls under a sort of spell. Current domestication induces a type of hypnotic trance that is shared and passed on from generation to generation. The dream is well hidden. Many people are unaware they're in a trance. They trust and believe their knowledge, their answers for how the world works.

The ancient wisdom phrase states the first people were free and they had questions. The first people are us as children. We live with questions. The answers we find in life are used to create our worldview. A worldview is a perception filter that guides us to seeing the world "our way". The answers we accept as true imprison us. We then become the second people. Our domestication trains us how to react to things in life and puts us in a sort of trance. We're unaware that we are not free. Feelings of powerlessness linger in the background as we try to find happiness. We use dysfunctional behaviors to cope and find some form of peace. The essence of recovery is to awaken and create new relationships with what we think is true.

My journey to light is a voyage of discovery, remembrance, inquiry and action. I discover how domestication holds me in prison. I remember how to look, and see with renewed innocence. I embrace inquiry and take action. I question my personal beliefs. Through inquiry I discover, remember and act toward change. It's a lovely adventure with amazing breakthroughs.

I first heard the ancient wisdom phrase about the 1st and 2nd people while attending a dreaming ceremony in Abiquiu, New Mexico. I carried this question in my consciousness for years, "Who are the third people?" Then one day while teaching a class an insight emerged. There on the clipboard was the wisdom phrase as the group engaged in an inquiry of how domestication limits our ability to be who we really are. These words came to me and completed the story.

"The third people gained freedom through inquiry."

Dear reader, you are the third people. Your journey is an inquiry to freedom from habitual patterns that don't nurture or sustain your true divine nature. The sleeping observer in us is awakened by questioning how we look at life. The quest for freedom from emotional suffering and discontent is done by embracing personal inquiry. As you practice the recovery principles you will develop a clear distinction between reacting to life by seeking answers and living in a state of inquiry. Questioning our knowledge opens us to possibilities. Welcome inquiry; release the shackles in your mind and journey to freedom.

PRINCIPLE

Awareness Lights the Path

"Awareness is the greatest alchemy there is. Just go on becoming more and more aware, and you will find your life changing for the better in every possible dimension. It will bring great fulfillment."

- Osho

Awareness is an ability to observe from an objective point of view; that's not personal or biased. It's the capability to witness from different viewpoints. Awareness is the power to control your attention. The terms mindfulness, alertness, wakefulness, cognizance and attentiveness also represent awareness. As a highly developed skill, awareness is the ability to perceive multiple perspectives simultaneously. Mastering awareness is a life-long process.

Someone once said to me, "I don't know what you mean by shifting perspective. I don't think I can do that. How can I look at things differently? I only have my point of view."

When working with groups I ask participants to do a simple exercise. First I ask, "Would you please do what I request and see what happens?" We are always free to choose. "If you agree to follow my instructions, I ask you to look at the ceiling and observe the patterns that are there to be seen." After a pause, I ask, "Please look at the floor and see the patterns that are there to be observed." Then I state, "Notice that when you're looking at the floor, your attention is on the floor and you can't see the ceiling. When you look at the ceiling, your attention is on the ceiling and you can't see the floor!" This is the nature of awareness; shifting perspectives and guiding your attention. I continue, "Now, notice you have been choosing to follow my commands. Please look at whatever you want. Place your attention on what you want to look at." After a pause I ask, "Is anyone not able to guide their attention and look at what they want?" After another pause I say, "Great! You have the basic skills necessary. Now you need to master the use of your talent."

Often the simplest examples carry great wisdom. I have yet to meet a human who doesn't have the potential to choose where they place their attention. Later in our group, it was discovered that when the person stated, "I only have my point of view," they were actually expressing unwillingness to change their point of view. We each have a unique perspective. Our viewpoints are not fixed, they can be shifted but it requires a willingness to shift.

Importance of Awareness

The condition of our world is directly related to the level of awareness in human consciousness. The status of our personal life shows how in touch we are with our creative powers. How much emotional turmoil do we create? How much of our life contains peace and tranquility? Are our relationships with others rich in empathy and connectedness? Or are they dominated by indifference and separation? What is the status of our physical health? Answering such questions tell us the state of balance between our spiritual, mental and physical aspects for whole health. And maintaining such an inquiry on a regular basis develops our awareness.

I do volunteer work with a nonprofit organization called Pachamama Alliance [3]. We are united in an effort to change the dream of the modern world. Our purpose is to bring forth an environmentally sustainable, socially just and spiritually fulfilling human presence on Earth. I facilitate presentations and have spoken with many people. I haven't met anyone who doesn't want a sustainable, just and fulfilling world. We all want the same thing. So why don't we create it?

We're not producing what we want because we lack awareness of how our actions impact the world. The collective human consciousness is in a sort of trance. We're not mindful of life's interconnectedness. If we were aware, we'd choose to do things that support the betterment of all. Unfortunately, our current systems sustain a world that is unjust, unsustainable and unsatisfying. The state of the world accurately reflects the level of awareness in the collective human consciousness. Developing our power of awareness is extremely important; now more than ever in human history.

Similarly, unhealthy personal behaviors continue in our life due to lack of awareness. We don't consciously seek to do harm through the use of drugs and alcohol. We want to cure the pain we feel. The idea that our relationships are being destroyed never occurs to us while we're using. We're ignorant to the consequences of our actions. Most of the time we blame others for the problems we see. Ignorance of outcomes from our behavior sustains dysfunctional behaviors. It's through awareness that we unearth what isn't working in our life. We examine the way we're approaching a situation and determine if it's making things better or worse. It's awareness that allows for healthy change to manifest.

Furthermore, the skill of awareness is very important for those who want to support others. Numerous counseling techniques exist and all of them work to develop cognizance of another person's perspective. Someone who's attentive to another's point of view is considered a terrific listener. Strong awareness skill promotes strong empathy and that nurtures understanding, connection and belonging. This leads to powerful healing potentials.

Whole Health Awareness

The three components for holistic health are **Body**, **Spirit** and **Mind**. Attentiveness is required to develop skills to support harmony among these three vital features of well-being. Awareness of our balance allows us to ride waves of sacred energy and align with the forces of life. Balance brings harmony. Alertness provides feedback for adjustment so we can stay on our board and ride life's flow.

Our **body** speaks and we can listen to the life in us with our attention. Every molecule and cell is alive. They all have functions that sustain our entire body. There is extraordinary communication transpiring with every breath we take. The collaboration required to simply breathe is very complex. Our body takes in air, filters it, absorbs nutrients, replaces oxygen with carbon dioxide, and then exhales. The teamwork is impressive; muscles talk to lung tissues and blood cells work with lung cells to support the health of the whole. It's an extremely complicated network with intimate cooperative relationships. Life functions we take for granted involve amazing communication between body, spirit and mind.

Awareness of our communication with our body directly affects health and quality of life. This was demonstrated during an open conversation in a support group I attended. The topic was early warning signs of mental illness symptoms. The group was sharing the physical experiences that occur. Stomach aches, racing heart, shallow breath, restlessness, loss of appetite and other physical sensations were recorded. I noticed how the group shared a common meaning about the words on the board that went something like: *these are signs of my mental illness.*

I said, "There's an interesting perspective being expressed by everyone. We've been describing what we feel in our body as a consequence of our diagnosis. We feel this or that because we have a mental disorder. My relationship with my body is different. I feel sensations and I hold it as my body talking to me, asking me to pay attention. My companion is guiding me and helping me to look at our condition and align spirit with mind. My body is helping me become aware that harmony is not present. From this perspective, my body is helping me become healthy by letting me know that attention is needed." Everyone's energy shifted as we changed perspective. It feels healthier to hold our body as a partner helping us rather than a sick, flawed thing.

We get valuable messages from the body. Massage, yoga, physical therapy and exercise support health. When combined with nutrition including macrobiotics we see great improvements in well-being. Then if we add spiritual and mental techniques that assist in harmony of the whole we see great advancements in healing. The body reflects the level of communion between Spirit and Mind.

Life and universal consciousness speak through **spirit**. Spirit is the silk that forms the web of life and connects everything.

There are no scientific methods to measure spirit. Therefore, many tend to overlook this important component of holistic health. Some of the greatest scientists have been profoundly spiritual. Einstein and Stephen Hawking may disagree on the meaning of the word "God" but they share respect for the marvel of consciousness communing with the unfolding of space and time. The thread of divine mystery that is sewn between matter and energy is light. Einstein's famous special theory of relativity states that energy is equal to mass times the speed of light squared ($E=MC^2$). Without going into science, let's explore the relationships and characteristics of matter, energy and light as represented in this equation. All matter has "form"; it has shape and texture. Energy has no form. Energy is "formless". Einstein's theory states that matter and energy are related to light. Another way to say this is matter and energy dance to light's heartbeat. Or form and formlessness twirl in the light of the universe. Matter and energy are connected through light. And guess what's in the light? ... Spirit!

Our body contains matter made by stars. It's composed of trillions of cells and each cell is made of trillions of atoms. Our body is the matter and our mind is the energy of our personal universe. And guess what connects our mind to the trillion-trillion atoms in our body? Yup! Spirit-Light connects it all. It's no coincidence that "spirit is light" is a common theme in most spiritual teachings around the world. The universe is connected through spirit-light or simply spirit. The mind and body connect through spirit in a similar way that energy and matter relate to light. Our body is the form that manifests out of the communion between mind and spirit.

Communion between spirit, body and mind is constantly occurring and how it all happens remains unknown. The mystery of life is the relationship between these vital components of life. How does all this relate to consciousness? Science is accumulating more evidence every day. The way science is thinking of consciousness is expanding. For example; Professor Suzanne Simard of University of British Columbia finds that old forest floors are actually interwoven communing systems of diverse forms of life that are interdependent to sustain life. They communicate through shared chemical and electrical signals. Mother trees send vital information and nutrients to younger trees and for the information to be passed a variety of other species assist. Suzanne Simard's research has discovered that forest life networks are organized much like the neural networks of our brain. Science is gathering evidence of Nature's consciousness. We are acknowledging symbiosis in the vast web of life and acknowledging what many indigenous traditions have known for generations. Everything is connected and consciousness is grandeur and more expansive than our separate individual minds. And the mysterious connector connecting it all is spirit.

The nature of spirit is mystery. It's the magic that animates life. Spirit is the light that resides between the stars and fills the space between atoms. It connects everything and is a part of everything. It also has no form so it is no-thing. We cannot accurately define it and explain it or measure it. That doesn't diminish it's grand significance. It is one third of the whole that nurtures health and vitality. Awareness of our spiritual relationships supports well-being.

Our **mind** is equally mysterious and fundamental for life. Thoughts and emotions emerge through our mind. They dance together relating and supporting each other. We think thoughts and emotions stir. We feel emotions and thoughts spring forth. They twirl to the beat of our life's song. Meanings and beliefs keep the beat. And we share it all with the universe.

Our mind uses two languages to communicate. Our mind is filled with words that make a spoken and written language. This allows us to communicate using symbols with shared meaning. Symbolic language is our mind's communion network that is based on forms that we call words. The other language we use contains no form. We share and communicate love, anger and many emotions. This language allows us to commune through an empathic language of feeling. Empathic language is the mind's communion network that is based on formless sensations we call feelings. The mind works simultaneously in both the form and formless dimensions using these two languages. Our mind is a crucial link between body and spirit.

Helen Keller's story provides validation to the importance of balance of spirit, body and mind. When she was 19 months old, she became deaf and blind from an unknown illness. She turned violent and uncontrollable. She had no language, no way to commune with her mind. Her teacher, Anne Mansfield Sullivan showed her how to share meaning through sign language. Helen Keller wrote, "As the cool stream gushed over one hand she spelled into the other the word water, first slowly, then rapidly. I stood still, my whole attention fixed upon the motions of her fingers. Suddenly I felt a misty consciousness as of something forgotten--a thrill of returning thought; and somehow the mystery of language was revealed to me. I knew then that "w-a-t-e-r" meant the wonderful cool something that was flowing over my hand. That living word awakened my soul, gave it light, hope, joy, set it free! There were barriers still, it is true, but barriers that could in time be swept away."[4] Helen Keller was spirit in a body without balance. When her mind received language, wholeness became possible. She used her awareness to pay attention and recover.

"The best and most beautiful things in the world cannot be seen or even touched. They must be felt with the heart."

\- Helen Keller

Eagle and Condor

Balance of mind and spirit exists when eagle and condor share the sky of our consciousness. The body reflects the balance with health, vitality and actions that nurture the continuity of life. What transpires in us personally shines out through light connecting us to the great web of life. So what we do for ourselves we do for the whole. Maintaining awareness of our state of balance between heart and mind, rational and intuitive, selfishness and generosity is watching our eagle and condor fly. As we restore balance to ourselves we support balance in our family, community, society and Mother Earth.

Eagle sight is a good representation for mental awareness. The eagle has amazing eyesight. Eagle can see features while soaring high. From great heights, the eagle sees detail and observes patterns in the terrain. An eagle can see a little mouse in tall grass while scanning the sky. Awareness, perception and attentiveness are the ways of eagle. Each of us can develop such awareness. Eagle sight allows us to witness the workings of our mind. We see how we create thoughts and emotions that manifest actions and consequences. Eagle eyes help us see detail of events and observe patterns in our life. As we gain height, we recognize shapes and trends. By stepping back and observing, we learn to fly and perceive things anew with a fresh perspective.

Condor flight is a wonderful symbol for sensory awareness. The condor flies high above Earth, effortlessly resting on currents. Condor glides with the energy available. Condor feels the air on its wings and adjusts ever so slightly to alter course. Sensory perception and sensing is what guides condor on life's journey. Relatedness and awareness of feelings unites condor with everything. Sacred sensations fill condor's sky. We can develop the awareness of condor by sensing how we feel as we react from habit. As we rise in altitude, we see patterns in our emotions. We recognize our relatedness to much more than our singular self. Our empathic abilities grow as we fly higher and we feel things in a deeper richer way.

Balancing the value of our mental abilities with our loving essence is the reunification of our eagle and condor. Our mind creates thoughts and emotions. Our heart resonates with the energy of love and life. We increase awareness by maintaining an inquiry of our state of harmony. We ask, "Are my emotions aligned with my heart and spirit? Are they emanating from heart felt love or are they coming from mind based fear?" We observe and adjust course as needed to maintain a state of grace that is in harmony with life.

Personal unbalanced conditions of unhappiness, dissatisfaction and emotional turmoil are mirrored in the condition of Mother Earth. We all seek harmony between Eagle and Condor. The purpose of recovery is to restore this healthy harmony to the whole. As we heal ourselves, we are healing our Mother.

Reflection Develops Awareness

Creating and maintaining harmony requires developing awareness so we can identify what is healthy and what brings forth discord. Awareness begins with reflection. All who work in behavioral health are working to increase awareness and help each other reach our full potential. Shery Mead founded Intentional Peer Support, IPS in the 1990's. "IPS is a process of experimentation and co-creation, and assumes we play off each other to create ever more interesting and complex ways of understanding."[5] Intentional peer support is an art form where the art supplies are communication skills. Instead of creating paintings or sculptures, practitioners create supportive healing conversations. Participants develop awareness as they learn how to grow healing relationships with others. Three key elements of peer support are: respecting worldview, building connection and recognizing mutuality. Through the coursework people write in journals and share what they're learning about themselves. All practices of peer support develop awareness by reflecting and expressing thoughts and feelings with others.

Substance abuse treatment and 12 step programs encourage people to share their story of addiction. Some groups ask members to write how they came to be addicted and the consequences that have occurred. Then they read their story to the group. This helps people understand personal feelings and thoughts about incidents in their life. During the process they relive events but from a new perspective. This time they are history writers. Story telling is a powerful healing tool. It helps people express suppressed and unexamined thoughts and emotions.

As we reflect, we are increasing our ability to shift perspectives. As we share and others listen, we create a cycle of giving and receiving. Mutuality manifests. And like cells working together to support the health of the body, we feel connected to the source of life. This is why peer support is so valuable. Healing happens when people express their pain and others compassionately accept what is shared.

We often have significant insights when we reflect on events. I have found that incredible clarity can appear and then vanish in a matter of minutes. I've lost amazing moments that I felt certain I would remember, only to have them disappear. That's why it's important to write or share what comes to you as soon as possible. Our minds are a conduit between form and formlessness. Thoughts appear and then fade away. When we record them we allow them to last longer. We can do this by writing or speaking what we discover. Placing our experiences into words helps create clarity and promotes remembrance. This is why journal writing is strongly recommended by behavioral health professionals.

Awareness/Mindfulness Practice

We enter the world innocent and very present to the moment. As our mind develops, we accept the answers given during domestication. We learn to play roles and focus on what everyone agrees is important. Over the years we fall asleep to our lullaby of knowledge. Awakening is a faster process but it needs regular practice. Body training requires commitment and exercise to create body strength. It also takes repetition to develop awareness muscles.

The behavioral health field uses the term, mindfulness to describe awareness. It means maintaining a moment-by-moment focus of our thoughts, feelings, bodily sensations, and environment. Practicing mindfulness can be done at any time. Most of my showers are active awareness exercise. I place all my attention on; the warmth of the water, the tingling sensations on my back and scalp, the slippery feeling of soap on skin. I pay attention to my attention and only on what is happening in the shower moment-by-moment. I become totally present to the sensations.

When I first started learning to take control of my reactionary mind, I set goals for my shower. Before stepping into the water I'd tell myself, "I'm not going to think of anything else. I'm only going to talk to myself about what I'm feeling in this moment." It would start great and I would feel so much. Then about mid afternoon I would remember what I had told myself before stepping into the shower. Hours had passed. "Where had I gone?" I wondered, "How did I loose my focus and shift away from the current moment?"

The next shower was better. I started fully present; feeling the sensations. Then I observed my mind wander. I noticed myself worrying about a bill that needed paying or what I must remember to do in the afternoon. I caught my attention drifting away from the sensations of the shower. My intent to remain present guided my attention back into the shower. I felt the warm water; the slippery soap, the moist air flowing through my nose. Then as I was drying myself with my towel, I'd notice I was planning what I would tell my friends when I saw them. I had returned to thinking and lost the second half of the shower experience. With practice, the amount of time I remain present while showering has significantly increased. And with it, my power of awareness in all areas of life.

Mindful showers are a great awareness training activity. A shower generally takes less than ten minutes. The sensations are strong and they are pleasurable. I challenge the reader to see how long they can stay present with their entire attention remaining on only shower sensations. It's surprising how much mind energy we use without knowing we are doing it. All hygiene activities can be treated as powerful mindful training exercises. Plus you'll have a much cleaner and happier body. Your body is your temple. It loves your attention.

The beautiful thing about mindful exercise is that you can do it while you walk, swim, bike or any activity. The key to accelerating awareness development is paying attention to where you are placing your attention. On a regular basis, create an intention to remain present to the moment. Seek to maintain this intent. Your mind follows your intent. When you notice your focus wandering off return your attention to the present moment and experience the sensations of what's happening now. With repetition, your ability to remain present improves. Your presence grows more powerful with practice. The more aware and attentive we are, the less we react to situations.

The ability to direct your attention is crucial for mastering awareness. Being mindful involves paying attention to all three aspects for health: spirit, body and mind. These qualities are interwoven. The thoughts we engage in are expressions of spirit and impact our body. Emotions such as anger and resentment stress the body. The feeling of our stomach tightening may be coming from our worry. Our mind speaks through both body and spirit. And emotions are a voice of the mind.

Emotions and the Mind

What is an emotion? What is a feeling? Are they the same or are they different? I love to examine the roots of words. The origin of words often provide insight. Emotion comes from the Latin word *emovere* which means "move out". Feel comes from the Old English word *felan* and means "to touch or have a sensory experience of; perceive, sense," The roots are quite different. Emotions are energetic waves that are "moving out ." What are they moving out from? They come from each of us.

We emote emotions and we feel feelings. We sense our emotions with our feelings. And because we feel emotions, we hold them as the same.

Awareness of our emotions can guide us on our journey. The condor in us allows us to sense our emotions. Condor feels currents of air. We feel the flow of our emotions. Warm air rises and cooler air falls. Condor rises up warm currents and avoids cold downdrafts to sustain flight. Condor's awareness allows this sacred creation to travel remarkable distances and soar to great heights. Air currents guide condor in flight. Our emotions also rise and fall. Maybe awareness of our emotions with wisdom will help us to soar as well.

Remember the difference in the roots "moving out" and "sense". Emotions move out. They are transmitted. We transmit or broadcast our emotions. The receptive qualities of our consciousness allow us to feel sensations. We receive/ sense with our feelings. Our emotions are like radio towers transmitting emotional energy waves. Our feelings are like satellite dish receivers receiving what is there to be felt. People are a lot like radio stations.

Radio and television news stations receive signals from around the world. Then the news staff looks at the information and defines what is and isn't important. They filter what is received. They interpret their perception and determine the relative meaning of what just came into the news room. We do the same thing with our perception. We feel and interpret what we see based on our acquired knowledge. Our worldview is like the editorial staff of radio station IM101-AM. After our filtering and interpretation, we broadcast our emotions into the universal airwaves. Others may pick up on what we emote or they may not. Maybe they're tuned to a different station or have their radio turned off. We all have experienced the feeling of not being received. There are also people who have their broadcast button stuck on without desire to receive the transmissions from others. One-sided biased news stations broadcast propaganda seeking to have their point of view accepted as the only way to see the world.

During my times of darkness, despair or discontent, I am unaware, listening only to my editorial staff. I let them choose to interpret my perceptions. Even though I hired them all, I let them run the newsroom. I am asleep and letting my worldview filter what I see and determine the emotions I will transmit. Gradually I became aware of this internal cycle of receiving, interpreting and broadcasting. Over the years I have fired numerous members of my personal editorial staff. The challenge of remaining awake in the midst of all the emotional broadcasting of humanity is why mastery of awareness is a life -long pursuit. And the rewards are well worth the time and effort.

Why do emotions exist? What is their function?

Nature travels through time with symbiosis as its captain. In Nature everything is related and interwoven in a vast web of life. Life eats life creating more life. Nothing is wasted in Nature. Everything serves the continuity of Life. This is seen at a microbial level and at the level of complex interdependent species. Small organisms are eaten by larger organisms to support their growth. Then large organisms are eaten by smaller organisms to nurture their decay. From Nature's perspective; everything exists to promote the continuity of Life. Within this context; why do emotions exist?

Eckhart Tolle wrote, "Emotion arises at the place where mind and body meet. It is the body's reaction to your mind — or you might say, a reflection of your mind in the body." [6] This is a wonderful starting place to help us understand why we have emotions and what is their purpose for supporting life. Our body reacts to the mind. Nature is wise and doesn't create without supporting the continuity of Life. We don't find anything wasted or without a purpose that supports Life. In Nature everything supports something else. We are a part of Nature and we create emotions. So emotions have a purpose that serves the continuity of Life. We merely need to embrace inquiry and discover how emotions serve Life.

Science tells us that we have five senses: sight, hearing, taste, smell and touch. Each is associated with a receiving part of the body: eyes/sight, ears/hearing, mouth/taste, nose/smelling, skin/touch. Each sense is a type of receiver. But we also receive emotions. The body empathically feels our mind through emotions. It appears science has missed a very important sense. Emotions are the sensory input that allows us to "feel our mind". In this case, our entire body is the receiver. So we would write the association for this sixth sense as body/emotion.

Emotions exist so we can taste our mind. The flavor of harmony is sweet and lovely. When mind, body and spirit are in harmony and the heart and mind align we are at peace with our emotions. Our experience of life falls into one of three categories when we are authentic, aware and fully present. We are either in a state of acceptance, enjoyment or enthusiasm.[7] We may not be enjoying what is happening but we're able to accept "what exists in this moment" and feel inner peace. When we're fully present, our emotions reflect our state and our feelings range from calm to joyful. Emotions are satisfying when we are in harmony with Life.

The taste of discord is bitter and ugly. When we're unaware and inauthentic; our experience is some level of unhappiness, discontent or emotional suffering. We don't like the emotions we feel in our body. Feeling anger or despair are not enjoyable experiences. We feel negative emotions because our mind is not in harmony with Life. Our body's ability to taste our mind and create a response is a beautiful creation of nature. Our body knows the deference between love and fear. When our mind is out of harmony with love, we feel an emotional reaction in our body. Our body monitors the state of harmony between heart and mind and displays an accurate emotion. Emotions are our personal mind alignment meter. We feel pleasurable emotions when our heart and mind align. We feel emotions we don't like when we our heart and mind are out of balance.

Emotional Guidance

How to use emotions to guide harmonious mental development will be taught in all the families of the future. Currently such understanding is not common knowledge or part of our domestication. Many of us struggle with our emotions and do the best we can with what we know. We create personal coping strategies to deal with undesirable emotions. Some methods are unhealthy and impede emotional maturity. We inhibit our emotional development when we use substances such as alcohol and drugs to suppress undesired feelings. Those recovering from alcohol and drugs know this well. When we stop using our substance of choice, we come face-to-face with unwanted emotions. Suddenly we no longer have our "medication" and the pain we don't want returns. We've been using for years. Now we have to find ways to cope on our own but we don't have emotional guidance skills. No wonder many people relapse and return to using a substance to escape unwanted pain. Our culture as a whole lacks understanding of how to support each other and grow through feelings with loving support. The recovery movement helps educate our culture so we can heal and grow in healthy harmonious ways.

Negative emotions are not something to be avoided, suppressed or feared. They are a beautiful creation of nature. When emotions are used with wisdom, they become a sense that guides us. The emotions we don't like are actually signals from the body letting us know that the mind is in discord with Life. They are a calling for us to align our mind with our heart. It is Nature's way of guiding us on our evolutionary path. Nature guides all life by providing signs with messages to follow. When elk smell the sent of wolf, alertness and attentiveness heighten. The elk's sense of smell delivers a message to pay attention and be alert. Similarly, negative emotions are how we smell danger coming from our mind. We are being told to pay attention to our state of harmony with Life. They are a mental alarm clock Nature created for us.

Negative emotions exist to help us wake up. They are like the rumble strips on a highway. Many American interstates have rumble strips, also known as sleeper lines that vibrate the car's tires hoping to awaken inattentive drivers. Similarly unpleasant emotions shout, "Wake Up! Pay attention to your attention! Align with love!" When we are alert, attentive, with a heart and mind in harmony, we are cruising down happiness highway. If we dose off and fall asleep we experience negative emotions helping us awaken. We are blessed with a self-correcting system for our mind. Negative emotions exist to help the mind develop and remain awake. They help us identify our level of presence, attentiveness, alertness and cognizance.

Our emotions are extremely valuable when we learn how to use them. The skill to develop is emotional guidance. This is using awareness of emotions to serve, guide and uncover shadows in the mind. Nature has provided us a beautiful mind alignment meter called emotion that allows us to develop our mind so it lives in harmony with spirit. Emotions are the songs sung by the duet of mind and spirit. Harmony resonates with peace and joy. Discord roars with anger and misery. As we feel our emotions we are listening to our mind and spirit sing. This book was written to help us learn how to harmonize our singers. Creating and maintaining harmony entails understanding and following the Eagle Condor Principles for Recovery.

In the not-too-distant future it will be common knowledge that our emotions serve to help us remain in balance with Life. Children will be raised and guided in how to listen to the heart and have the mind remain in alignment with love. At school, children will be taught of the difficult times their ancestors faced. A teacher may say, "Our ancestors lived in very difficult challenging times. They believed that happiness was outside of themselves. They didn't know like we know now that we are happiness. Love is the natural way of Life. They were afraid and tried to suppress their emotions because their world was dominated by fear. It was a scary place where people struggled and fought for control."

A new world will exist when we treat emotions as a sense of the body and support each other in how to use our emotional sense to align our mind with spirit. People will create beautiful art using their emotions like we do our other senses. People will support each other and strive for harmony together. Such a world is our destiny. It aligns with the universal light in each of us.

Attitude is the Emotion-Thought Interface

Attitude is a settled way of thinking and feeling that is reflected in our behavior. Negative attitude is detrimental to our health and vitality. Whereas a positive attitude encourages healing and opens the door to new possibilities. Attitudes are grown like plants in a garden. They become strong and have a life of their own. A positive attitude is like a lovely morning glory blooming and welcoming the morning sun. A negative attitude is like thorny, parasitic vines inhibiting life around them while living off a host plant. Parasites weaken the host as they feed. Similarly, health declines for those with a negative attitude.

Consciousness is mirrored in nature and reflected in all life. Microscopic cells interact with their environment in ways similar to how attitudes relate to our world. Cells float in a sea of nutrients and potential toxins. Cell membranes allow materials into the cell. Healthy membranes only allow nutrients in while preventing toxins from entering. Similar to cells, we float in a sea of emotions. Some are positive/nurturing while others are negative/toxic. Our attitude is like a cell-membrane that allows thoughts to feed emotions. A positive attitude is like a healthy cell-membrane allowing healthy thoughts to feed healthy emotions. A negative attitude allows toxic thought to feed harmful emotions. Negative attitudes align with poisonous emotion and thought that contaminate our body.

Changing attitude is like a snake shedding its skin. The snake feels a calling and accepts that it must transform to grow. An inner knowing emerges saying, "Now is the time." The snake intuitively knows the old skin must go in order to remove parasites and grow. The same is true for us. Life sings its song asking us to transform and evolve. Inside we feel a calling that now is the time to change. We recognize that our attitude is not supporting our true potential. An inner knowing emerges that it is time to shed our parasitic thoughts and emotions. It's time to transform and create a healthy attitude.

Moving from pessimism to optimism doesn't happen overnight. It requires work and commitment. There are numerous methods to develop skills to avoid negative thinking that promote harmful emotions. Here are a few;

- Still your mind using meditative/mindful techniques.

- Change your focus by placing your attention on something that is supportive and healthy.

- Surrender your worries. Put them away and don't waste your energy worrying.

- Embrace acceptance of "what is" without judgment.

- Practice gratitude. Opening yourself to feeling grateful shifts your perception instantly.

- Reframe your struggles; see your situation as growing pain. Your weathering a storm like a young seedling. You're a snake shedding its skin.

- Use your body to help you get in touch with your life force.

- Let go and unwind your resistance to change.

- Practice Loving Kindness Meditation (LKM) on a regular basis. Such meditations support loving acceptance of yourself, others and all creation.

A fundamental truth of life is that we want to be well. Our cells want to be healthy. Life wants to live through us. We are here to exist in harmony like every other life form. This root truth permeates everything. At the core of it all is love. The force that keeps everything going is love. When we align with love, our attitude transforms and compassion, collaboration, peace and joy emerge. This allows for positive attitudes to grow naturally. When Spirit, Body and Mind are in harmony; our attitude flows with positivity and possibility. We recover our natural way of being. We're authentic. We're how we were meant to be.

Awareness is the Beacon for Communion

Communion is a simple and beautiful term. It's definition is; "sharing intimate thoughts and feelings, especially when the exchange is on a mental or spiritual level." Sharing of intimate thoughts and feelings creates deep connections. Typical conversations exchange thoughts and feelings. But communion carries a level of intimacy that has strong healing potential. Powerful support groups and therapy sessions manifest when rich communion is present. Sharing intimacy allows us to connect through love without calling it Love. The free exchange of personal thoughts and feelings supports healing through acceptance. When we're allowed to express what we feel and sense its reception, we align with the consciousness of others . Communion is a strong deep conscious connection that is profound. It's special because it's intensely spiritual.

When we pray, meditate and go for walks in nature; we commune with Life that is greater than ourselves. Universal consciousness is in a continual state of communion through an infinite network of thoughts and feelings. Communion is ongoing and everlasting. It occurs at an individual level between a unique Mind, Body and Spirit and at a much grander level of universal connectedness. When we stand before a tall majestic tree and ponder the years it has lived and all it has seen, we open our mind to receive intimate sensations from the natural world. Sitting and meditating or praying connects our mind to the vast consciousness of all life.

Awareness is like a brightly shining lighthouse beacon. It lights our space allowing us to commune with life. The light of awareness reveals patterns and intimate detail that were hidden in darkness. Our level of awareness, our brightness, determines the depth, richness and intimacy of our experience. We commune with the magic of the moment as we savor a sunset. It draws our attention and guides our communion. The greater our attentiveness and ability to feel, the more powerful our connection to universal consciousness. Awareness is our beacon for communion. It allows us to connect to greater powers and see what is in shadow.

Awareness Lights the Path (Revealing Shadows)

Each of us is a shining light of infinite potential when we enter this world. As we grow we learn how to confine our light and conform to the wishes of others. We innocently believe what grown-ups say and we believe their answers to our questions. As children, we are the "first people" full of wonder and free of the confines of what we think is true. We become the "second people" as we mature and join society sharing such beliefs as; *economic growth is good, owning things makes us happy, money creates security, seeking more than you need is natural, monetary wealth provides freedom.*

Many of us use substances to deal with emotional distress. Some of it is obtained from a doctor with a prescription; some find help from a cocktail served at a tavern. Others find what they need from sweets at the grocery store. We all savor relief from emotional turmoil as we enjoy our favorite "spirit" helper. Consuming behavior increases as we seek to survive in our dysfunctional world. We act to relieve our pain and suffering without awareness of why we're seeking escape. Unhealthy behaviors continue because of beliefs such as; *I can quit whenever I want. This isn't bad, at least I'm not out of control like those addicts. I have good reasons to use. My using isn't hurting anyone. I only do it once in awhile.* Such ideas are reasons to maintain the status quo and justify our actions. They encourage a lack of awareness of consequences. The truth is, actions of addiction negatively impact life. The individual with addiction is not aware of the negative effects they're creating. And believing certain ideas helps conceal adverse consequences.

Our body works to restore balance whenever we have a cut or bruise. Nature seeks health and vitality. The natural desire of the molecules and cells in our body is harmonious balance that sustains life. Unhealthy behaviors go against this natural instinct in our body. Therefore, we need to participate in some form of deception in order to sustain harmful activates. We unconsciously create beliefs to justify actions that go against our natural instincts. This practice develops a sense of apathy that numbs our ability to sense we are doing something unhealthy. Apathy helps sustain dysfunction because its easier to go against natural instincts if we don't care. Our justifications create an illusion that we're not doing harm. We create a worldview that believes something like; *It's ok. I'm just doing what I must to survive*. We don't look any deeper to see if harm is being done to ourselves or others. If we did, we would loose our sense of "being right" or "doing what's best". Mental deception within our mind is how addictive behaviors sustain their existence. It's how they remain in shadow, away from the prying eye of our authentic self; the spirit within.

Most of the modern world suffers with addictions. Our consumptive ways are destroying habitat and polluting the planet. Wildlife is going extinct at an unprecedented rate. Climate change is occurring. Our modern way of life promotes apathy. Many with more than they need prefer not to know about the state of poverty, environmental degradation and pollution. *I have it good and I'm not the cause of this*, is a common unexamined assumption in modern society. Apathy is required for humanity to continue on its current course. If we saw the truth of our relatedness, we'd change our behaviors. We believe we're doing what's best while we damage our world. Our culture shows all the symptoms of addiction. We deny that our way of life is causing harm to ourselves and others. The truth is; everything is connected.

Awareness is the light that illuminates what needs to be seen for harmony with life to be restored. Deceptive thoughts are revealed. Unexamined assumptions are examined and new perspectives become available as we awaken. The impact of our addictions are becoming apparent and undeniable. The modern way of life is facing transition. We are being asked to examine how our way of life is affecting all life on the planet. We are being called to face the fact that we have consumption addictions. We need to embrace inquiry and question what we have been assuming is true. We are not alone and we are related to everything on this planet.

Dependency looses its hold when the light of awareness is bright. Those of us who are choosing to live in recovery and accept the challenge of creating a new way of living are the ancestors of future generations. We are the ones who will shift from old habitual dysfunctional habits to loving and sustaining activities. As we heal ourselves from our disharmony, we heal the world. As we awaken others awaken. Everything is evolving. A great awakening is occurring and all life is a part of a grand new emerging world. The light of truth is in each of us. Awareness allows the light to shine forth and brighten the path.

A magnificent wild creation was slaughtered by human apathy and arrogance while I was writing this section. A dentist from Minnesota traveled to Zimbabwe, Africa and killed a 13 year old male lion named Cecil. The event sparked great controversy and displayed two vital points. The act itself shows humanity's apathetic and narcissistic attitudes toward other life on Earth. The outrage in the media and by the public displayed evidence of the awakening in humanity's consciousness. Not long ago, there would have been little to no outcry. We are moving from an apathetic to empathic relationship with Life. Empathy needs to be nurtured and promoted. A calling to care for each other and Earth is being sung in the light. It resonates deep within, asking us to remember the sacredness of all things. We are recovering our true divine nature as we work to free ourselves from the illusion that we are not sacred. Human awareness and empathy are what the world needs at this time to heal.

Awareness / Mindfulness Exercises

Awareness is the art of observation. Through the act of maintaining awareness, you are learning how to control your conscious power of intent that guides your presence and directs your attention. Practice involves participation with the sensory inputs of your human form. Our body delivers sensations through our eyes, ears, touch, taste, and smell. We master awareness by placing our attention on what we feel in the moment. You can practice at any time, whenever you remember the importance of being present and developing your awareness skills. Here are some examples to help you get started. You are encouraged to create other ways that serve your personal journey of discovery.

Awareness while eating

Before you honor your body with nourishment, reflect on the food before you. Become aware of the aliveness that is about to become a part of you. Simply be with and feel the connection between the life that you are and the life that will soon be a part of you. For a moment reflect and acknowledge that what you are about to eat carries life force energy. You are about to participate in the process of transformation. Feel gratitude for the life transfer.

Use all your senses, feel the chair you sit on. Feel the knife and fork in your hand. Feel the warmth of the food. Feel the smoothness of the plate and cup. Smell the aroma. Take in the flavors through your nose before the first bite. Witness the colors. Is there steam rising? Feel the texture of all the surfaces your body touches. Observe all sounds.

Continue savoring each sensation. Taste with every cell you can sense. Use all your senses to their fullest extent. Record what you experience and observe.

Awareness during hygiene activities

Our body is our vessel for the duration of our time in human form. It is a sacred container for it carries a divine presence that is our essence. Honoring our body honors our cellular dimension and nurtures our aliveness. Tending to our body supports our well-being.

Whenever you bathe, shower, shave, brush your teeth and comb your hair, make the activity into a practice of awareness. Place your complete attention into the sensations. Become aware of your mental activities and maintain a focus on the sensations.

These are nice times to express your desire to honor and respect yourself. This is when you can be with you and witness the company you keep with yourself. Are you loving to your body? Do you hold your vessel in high esteem? If not, are you willing to? Do not dwell in internal conversation. Now is not the time. Now is the time to be present to the moment and feel and observe and express sensations experienced. Use all your senses to their fullest extent. Record what you experience and observe.

Awareness with the breath

The sacredness of each breath is an overlooked gateway to inner peace. As we breathe we are performing the most basic elemental function of life. With each breath we are in communion with all other life forms on this planet. Air is a vehicle of communion with life in the physical dimension. When we breathe in, we receive life giving oxygen that our body requires. The oxygen that we take in has been prepared for us with love by other life forms. Our partners on earth, the plants, have carefully prepared oxygen for us. With each out-breath, we deliver to the plant world our carbon dioxide that has been prepared by us for our partners in life, the plant kingdom.

Each breath is a dance of love between us and all our partners in life.

Just think, the air you have just taken into your lungs was once circling the Andes mountains. The oxygen you now have within you was once a part of the Pacific Ocean swirling and then splashing against the rocks of the Hawaiian Islands evaporating into the sky and dancing among the clouds, and swirling down to earth to enter your body with that last breath!

Whenever the desire emerges to be still or find some peace, return to your breath and practice the skill of awareness. Place your attention on your breath. Feel the sensation of air entering. If your mind is active, choose to change the conversation and make the self talk about what you are experiencing as you breathe. Describe to yourself the air coming in, is it cold or warm? Is it moist or dry? What sensations is your body feeling as you witness your breath? Expand your awareness of your sensations as you become more and more present to the sensations of your body while you dance the most basic steps of life. Use all your senses to their fullest extent. Record what you experience and observe.

Awareness of aliveness in your body

Feeling the aliveness in your body is an incredibly powerful tool for healing and developing your ability to become totally present. Our body is composed of billions of cells interconnected and communicating every moment. You can learn to feel your body and take your attention wherever you desire. It can be a fantastic healing encounter when you become skilled at maintaining your presence within your body. This exercise is an introduction to help you learn how to feel the life force that is you.

This is best done in a still room with no air currents. Sit or stand with your arms freely hanging at your side. Adjust yourself so your hands are not touching anything. Guide your attention by asking yourself a simple question, "How can I tell if my hand is still connected to my body without moving it or touching anything?" Place your focus on feeling the sensations in your hand. Be patient and persistent with intent to feel for the presence of your hand. Use all your attention to feel the feeling that is your hand.

The sensation is like a glowing or humming feeling. It feels like vibrations at a very high frequency and yet this description fails to capture the total feeling. Go deep into the sensation of your hand. Feel what your hand feels like from within. Maintain your focus on the feeling. If you find yourself struggling with thoughts like, *this is stupid; What's the point?* Let those thoughts pass. That's just your mind wanting your attention. Keep your attention on feeling your hand and finding ways to describe the feelings to yourself. Once you are successful at feeling your hand, notice the state of your mental activity. How still is your mind?

Loving Kindness Meditation (LKM)

In the sacred writing of the Buddha can be found the saying: "Hatred cannot coexist with loving-kindness, and dissipates if supplanted with thoughts based on loving-kindness." Loving Kindness Meditation is a wonderful practice to help shift attitude. It also is a wonderful practice to help you get in touch with the sacredness of life on a regular basis. The basic idea is to spread good, loving intention to yourself and others. You begin with creating a mantra of a desired blessing for yourself such as; *May I be happy. May I be healthy.* May I be filled with peace. Sit comfortable. Take a few deep breathes and still your mind. Then follow these steps:

1. Visualize yourself and repeat the phrase several times; *May I be happy.*

2. Visualize a beloved (dear friend or family member) and repeat the phrase with their name replacing "I" in the mantra; *May Janet be happy.*

3. Visualize someone you truly feel neutral about and repeat the mantra with their name inserted. Be sure they are someone you neither like or dislike. Often this is challenging because we tend to judge most people either good or bad.

4. Visualize someone you dislike and repeat the mantra with their name. Learning to send love those we do not like or who have harmed us can be incredibly freeing and empowering.

5. Expand your vision outward to include, your community, country, all people and all life everywhere. Repeat the mantra when you are ready to send a blessing to the universe; *May all beings everywhere be happy.*

It's important to think through the process before beginning. Then while meditating deeply feel the blessing and love being sent by you to yourself, to your beloved, the one you feel neutral toward, the one you dislike and all life. This practice heals much pain and summons the power of love as your ally. It is a wonderful tool for shifting attitude and nurturing compassion, empathy and awareness.

CHAPTER THREE

Drama's Relentless Cycle

"… for there is nothing good or bad, but thinking makes it so. To me it is a prison. "

William Shakespeare: Hamlet, Act II Scene 2

William Shakespeare was a master of theatrical drama. His plays present human conflict with riveting entertainment. In Shakespeare's play, Hamlet, the main character, is visited by a ghost and learns that his uncle murdered his father and married his mother. Hamlet thinks obsessively about his situation. Thinking about what he knows and judging things were a prison for Hamlet. The knowledge Hamlet bore imprisoned him in a chronic state of revenge. There is no transformation, no recovery, in Hamlet. All characters play their roles and the cycle of drama leads to a tragic end with the death of the entire royal family.

Living life in drama; stuck in roles, controlled by habitual patterns, without transformation, condemns us to repeat mistakes over and over. Many of us live life through dramatic roles, captured by our thinking, unaware that human conflict is draining our spirit. Most of humanity's suffering comes from tragic performances played out in real life.

While I worked as a peer support specialist within the behavioral health system, I had the opportunity to observe drama from both recipients of service and staff. One day I was given a wonderful chance to directly observe a colleague suffer in the prison of her thinking.

It was a beautiful Sunday morning. I stood in the kitchen of the Learning and Recovery Center enjoying my wake-up, begin-my-shift cup of coffee. Sipping quietly I listened to the latest reports on everyone's life situation. I was informed that Nadine was not at the center. That was very odd because she was very reliable and assigned to be on duty.

"Where's Nadine?" I asked.

"She called and will be late because her dog, Mia is missing. She's out looking for her and will be in as soon as she can." a peer explained.

Moments later, Nadine entered the center.

"Did you find your dog?" I asked. There was no need to ask the question. Her facial expression and body language told me she was carrying a heavy burden.

"No!" was her response. Displaying great pain and sorrow she continued, "I'm sorry, I don't mean to sound bitter. I've looked everywhere. I've had the sheriff over and he's looking too." Tears filled her eyes as she worked to hold herself together.

No words could be said to relieve the sense of grief charging the air. There was no escape. Nadine filled every room she entered with sadness and sorrow. The center became a funeral home with a wake in progress.

As the morning crept along Nadine continued sharing her thoughts and emotions. She was certain Mia had been hit by a car and hobbled under a bush and was hiding out of sight. Nadine knew that her beloved puppy was lying in pain, whimpering and slowly dying in agony. Unable to let go of her tragic drama, she suffered in her prison created by what she thought was true.

After hours of exhausting worry, the phone rang. A caller asked for Nadine. Words shared over a telephone transformed the energy of the center and everyone's experience of life. Nadine's eyes widened and great joy flowed as she heard the true story of Mia's exploratory morning. The puppy had gone to a neighbor's house and shared a delightful savory visit. Mia got to taste wonderful foods and feel the love of children as their parents searched to find the puppy's owner. Mia's real adventure was glorious and filled with joy. Nadine's was a dark contrast full of emotional pain and anguish. Hamlet said, "there is nothing good or bad, but thinking makes it so." A puppy enjoyed a pleasant morning as Nadine's thinking made it bad.

Nadine lived a morning of intense drama that impacted her health and the environment of everyone she was near. She drained herself and those who shared her drama. It was an amazing experience to watch unfold. I saw drama exhausting everyone. Then a remarkable release of joy and freedom highlighted the power of our mind to direct energy. The roles we play guide how we use our valuable life energy. Nadine played the role of a grieving mother for hours and everyone felt the emotions from the death of a child. All her painful sensations were real. But the source of the pain, her story, was make believe. She performed her role so well it would have won an award if done on stage. Our conversation afterwards provided incredible learning as she saw for the first time how she played out a drama of her creation. It was an insightful moment that opened her door to transforming how she relates to what she assumes is true.

"How can I stop creating such drama in my life?" Nadine asked.

I replied, "By developing awareness, stepping out of drama and sustaining your intent to change. Each step requires skills that are developed with practice. You learned a valuable lesson today. You got to feel what it's like when you assign meaning to what you imagine is true. Then you felt the great freeing sensation you get when you release your attachment to what you believe. Imagine if you let go of all the drama in your life. The feeling of freedom is far greater than what you felt today when you discovered Mia was alive and well."

Amazing shifts occur when people stop participating in drama. People experience a sense of peace that is very attractive. Once we get a taste of life without dragging our emotional baggage around, we want more freedom. There's an interesting trend occurring in all of us. People in general are altering their relationship to role playing. Many commonly shared beliefs are losing their appeal. During Shakespeare's day, everyone agreed that revenge was the obvious natural reaction to wrong doing. The notion of "an eye for an eye" has been passed on from generation to generation for eons. Our need for revenge is slowly fading and is evidenced by countries removing death penalty laws.

There is a great turning occurring in humanity's consciousness and it is showing itself in our relationship with drama. The days of defining each other based on the roles we play is softening. The decay of drama's acceptance in everyday life is connected to our desire for equal rights. We want to connect and feel like we are being treated fairly. Personal roles are changing as we write new parts for us to play.

One of the new roles emerging is someone learning the process of recovery. As we practice mindfulness and increase our power of awareness, we develop the capacity to change how we see things and choose different actions. Before Nadine's dramatic experience with her dog and our inquiry together, she had no idea she was a victim of her thinking. Nadine realized how making assumptions and taking things personally were creating her unhappiness. She saw clearly how she was imprisoned by what she thought was true. For the first time in Nadine's life, she discovered that her thinking was causing her great despair. With that insight, she was given the opportunity to step out of her persistent drama cycle. Nadine felt hope for a new way of being with her mind and began serious practice of the recovery principles.

Learning how to transform is mastering personal change. When we practice transformation, we move away from unhealthy patterns that diminish our experience of life and replace them with behaviors that nurture our well-being. Recognizing what needs to shift comes with awareness. Taking action that creates change is transformation.

For transformation to occur we must become aware of what isn't working. This allows us to identify what needs to change. Drama can be entertaining when performed on stage and in film. It can be very wasteful and destructive when played out in a person's life. Vast amounts of human suffering are created from our addictions to drama, making assumptions, taking things personally and seeking agreements to justify it all. All of it is a misuse of precious life force energy and it's exhausting.

So why do we waste our energy doing such crazy things? Well, we do it because of innocent ignorance. We do it because everyone else is doing it and we believe it is "normal". What would the world be like if living in drama wasn't "normal"?

It is possible to live without creating drama in your life. And it's a wonderful, fulfilling and free way to live. Freedom comes through inquiry. It's time to explore the drama cycle and see how it plays out in our life so we can become aware and transform how we think of things.

In the next section, we're going to explore the basic elements of the drama cycle and see how they appear in our life. With understanding, comes opportunity to transcend drama's relentless destructive cycle.

PRINCIPLE

Presence Transcends Drama

"I never travel without my diary. One should always have something sensational to read in the train."

- Oscar Wilde

Webster's dictionary defines drama as: a composition which tells a story, usually of human conflict, by means of dialogue and action, to be performed by actors. Most of humankind lives life in drama unaware that we're acting out a play of our creation. The story of humanity is rich in human conflict performed by generations of actors. We have heroes, villains and victims throughout recorded history. Many mythologies tell of divine beings driven by drama. Human conflict triggers reaction that has us perform repeating behaviors based on roles we've learned from others. Sons act like fathers. Daughters act like mothers. We pass down our dramatic roles from generation to generation.

Our personal story becomes dramatic when we fill it with meaning. Most of us mistake our story for reality. We assume our perceptions and interpretations are accurate and judge our situation. This allows us to justify how we feel about things. We take things personally and generate emotions. An illusion filled with dramatic events consumes our senses and we react assuming this is the truth of life. We share the drama and spread it to others. However, deep inside we sense the drama isn't "real". This is why we seek agreements with others. Our story is validated and "proven real" when others agree with us. Agreements are necessary to keep the illusion of drama "real". The human drama cycle rolls on, perpetuated by people agreeing with imagined explanations. The wheel keeps going round and round like a merry-go-round we ride; never realizing we can get off at any time.

The story of Nadine's lost dog highlights these points. Nadine assumed she knew what had happened to her beloved dog, Mia. Her sharing of her drama nurtured agreement from others as the meaning of the terrible loss spread through the recovery center. It was in fact a complete illusion but the feelings and sensations were alive and experienced by everyone.

We're given an opportunity to rise above patterns of behavior that have imprisoned us for generations when we see how drama plays out in our life. When we see the drama cycle for what it is — a world of make believe — we become free to step out and walk the path of our choosing. Understanding the cycle and its elements allows us to recognize it as an illusion and freely choose alternative ways to be with our situation.

The Drama Cycle

Habitual ways of looking, seeing, feeling and reacting are symptoms of an active drama cycle. The cycle can also be thought of as a wanting cycle. Wanting more things, wanting happiness, wanting others to like me, wanting to look a certain way, wanting another drink or a fix; these are all signs of a drama cycle. The cycle is an endless loop of never having enough. Addicts know this well. Anyone suffering from a compulsive habitual pattern knows the feeling of needing to have. It's insatiable wanting.

The drama cycle runs continuously. People play out drama at work and at home. Some people have drama in their intimate relations and not with their friends. Others engage in drama with neighbors and not co-workers. Work, romance, health, family and all areas of life can have drama. Cycles play out with different performers. Our life has an abundant cast of characters playing numerous roles. However, when we step back and look, we can see similarities in what may appear unrelated events.

To help us see how the drama cycle works; we begin with a want. Imagine a child wants a bicycle. What happens next? Maybe the child takes action such as asking their parents. Perhaps they just daydream and hope their bike will appear as a holiday or birthday gift. Such dreaming is wanting without physical action. So, the child either acts or they don't act. What happens next? A consequence appears as a result of the child's action. The result is a new situation with two possibilities; the child gets a bike or they don't.

The first three stages of the cycle are as follows; a want appears in our mind, we either take action or not, a result then manifests and we either get what we want or we don't get what we want. These steps of the cycle are presented in the figure below. They are: Want, Action/No Action and Result/Situation.

Start of Drama Cycle

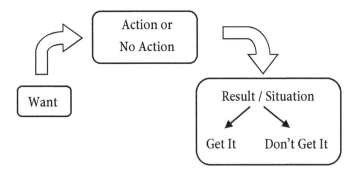

During the initial stages of the cycle, we behave in a similar fashion to other creatures in nature. A want appears; animals get hungry and search for food. Action is taken with a result; they either find food or remain hungry. Another desire manifests followed by action; urges to find a mate appear and ritual activities begin. A situation results; a mate joins in the ritual or not. In the plant world, roots grow stretching through the soil seeking minerals. Nutrients are found or not. The pattern of desire followed by action and result is seen throughout nature. Notice, there is no drama. It's a simple process of having a desire, taking action and either getting what you want or not getting it. Having desire is natural. Even single cell organisms get hungry and seek food. These three basic stages happen everywhere in nature.

A lion's hunger calls and the skillful hunter stalks an unsuspecting gazelle. With silent precision the lion lingers in a perfect location. The wind is right, the tall grass excellent cover. The gazelle is highly aware and attentive. There in the meadow, two lives are alert and present. They tune into the buzz from a bumble bee's wings as it gathers nectar at a nearby flower. Each step the gazelle takes arouses the lion's senses, its muscles tense in preparation for release. A crow caws as muscles spring. The gazelle dashes; startled by the bird's cry. The prey escapes. The lion pauses; smelling for other opportunities. The lion didn't get what it wanted. Hunger remains. The lion moves on.

Creatures of nature take the result obtained as the answer in harmony with the universe. They accept the situation and move on. Maybe they pursue the same want or their desire shifts and they rest with no action. Nature doesn't demonstrate dramatic conflict. There is only a want, action and result —a simple cycle without drama. This is nature's way.

Humans don't end the cycle at this point. We're much more creative! We have wants, actions and results just like all of nature but then people do something unique. We process the situation with our mind. We analyze it. We create judgments and determine the significance of what just happened. Then we assign meaning to the situation. This forms an attachment between us and the meaning we just created. We identify with the result and take it personally. This gives the situation a measure of worth. Grasping how we assign meaning, form attachments and identify with events in our life is key to understanding why we do what we do.

Assigned Meaning and Related Emotion

Let's say the child asks mom for a bicycle and hears the answer, "No." The next question from the child would be, "Why?" This is the child's attempt to assign meaning to the unwanted result - "no". Suppose mom answers, "Because you'll hurt yourself!" She is concerned for the child's safety and with the traffic in the area; she has sound reasons to be cautious. However the child may think, *Mom doesn't trust me. She thinks I'm unable to ride. I'm useless.* The child is making assumptions and taking it personally in order to make sense of the situation. A feeling of knowing emerges in the child. We make assumptions and assign meaning to develop a sense of understanding of the situation. We want to feel like we know what's going on. We begin doing this innocently when we're young and continue the same process as adults without awareness that we're doing it.

The meaning and attachment we give to a situation has two basic qualities; the situation is either good or bad. How good or bad it is depends on how attached we are to the situation. If we have taken it very personally, it carries a very high level of attachment. If we're not close to what happened, it has little charge. The amount of meaning and attachment we feel is a measure of our identification with drama.

After taking the result personally, we manifest emotions related to our assigned meaning of the result. The extent of emotions is vast. They range from severe anger and frustration to extreme excitement and gaiety. Our emotion generation is directly related to our attachment to the events transpiring. The intensity or power of our reaction is tied to how much personal energy we devote to the meanings we believe are true. Our assigned meaning contains our judgement. If the situation is acceptable, we express some form of happiness. When the result is unacceptable, we generate various degrees of unhappiness. The strength of our emotion is related to the level of personal investment we have assigned to our meaning of the situation.

Imagine the lion's thoughts if he lived in drama. After chasing the gazelle through tall grass and becoming exhausted, the lion might think, *That damn crow! Why did she have to do that and mess up my life! I hate crows. They're always cawing at the wrong time and never know when to shut up! I'm hungry and pissed off! I need to let off some steam. I think I'll shred this bush. How come I have to do all the work! Stupid crow!*

But, we don't see such story telling in the actions of animals. Unless we watch animated movies that personify nature and show us how we live in drama. Most of nature doesn't appear to make assumptions or take things personally in order to assign meaning to what is happening. These are human characteristics that we teach each other.

The cycle of drama contains simple elements that are easily identified. When I first recognized this cycle and saw how it played out over and over in my life, I was astounded. It shows how we interact with the world. The diagram below shows the entire drama cycle.

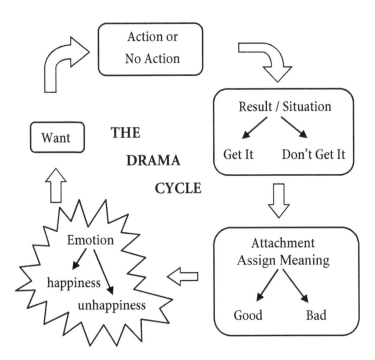

Nadine's lost dog drama illustrates the cycle. She wanted to know her puppy was safe. She took action by searching the neighborhood, calling friends and talking to the sheriff. She didn't get what she wanted. Then Nadine assigned meaning. She created a horrific story of slow death of a puppy by the roadside under bushes. It had a very "bad" meaning that grew emotions of grief, loss and unhappiness. Nadine was trapped for hours in a dramatic story that she created.

As another example imagine this scenario. You feel nervous and anxious worrying about your life situation. Sleeping is a challenge. You want relief. Enticing thoughts emerge telling you; *This time will be different. You've been sober for weeks. You've proven that you have things under control.* You use your substance of choice and find relief. The calm you wanted has returned. You got what you wanted. You feel in control. Life has meaning and you're happy. Then the substance induced euphoria wears off removing the sense of happiness. The wanting for relief returns and the cycle repeats. Chemical dependency is the same vicious cycle.

The assigned meanings we create are the links of a chain that attach us to stories that we believe are true. Most of us are unaware that we're forming attachments. We're simply trying to make sense of what we're experiencing. As we develop awareness, we learn how to use keys that release our attachment to assumptions and interpretations. The keys to freedom have numerous forms.

There are many methodologies to help us escape the relentless cycle of drama. The practice of "positive thinking" works to encourage "good" meaning to events. It aligns our attachment toward optimism. Finding the silver lining in a situation assigns a positive point of view. Stress management techniques that induce relaxation help us let go of our attachment to stressors. Breath work, massage and other practices release us from attachments stored in our body. Many of the eastern spiritual teachings such as Buddhism emphasize quieting the mind. Meditation creates a space between our life situation and our thoughts and concerns. And most religious doctrines promote giving up attachment to material things.

The drama cycle shows all possibilities in a generalized form. This makes it easier to understand relationships. For example, we can see that there are two ways to create unhappiness in life. The obvious one is; we don't get what we want. But there's another way. We can get what we want and this can lead to unhappiness. People strive, working hard to obtain their goals expecting to find happiness. Then they get what they always wanted. But they feel hollow, empty and unhappy. This can happen if we believe: *Things will bring us happiness.* History contains numerous famous wealthy people committing suicide. People obtain fame and fortune only to find emptiness and dark despair. The drama cycle can lead to death when we fully invest our faith in it.

It's important to note that the drama cycle doesn't have a beginning or an end. It is a continuous loop going round and round. Cycles have short and long episodes. Some cycles are slow and others are fast. For example; finding a job may be a long cycle taking months or years. While you search you may have racing thoughts about your situation, that cycle is very fast. Each thought can be an action that doesn't change the situation yet increases attachment that nurtures a growing emotional charge. Recall a sensation when you worried about a problem. Remember how the feeling of anxiety increased as you repeatedly thought about it. That is a drama cycle spinning and generating more emotion. The chemical dependency scenario is another example of drama whirling inside and increasing the desire to use a substance. As the cycle whirls thoughts emerge and alter meanings making the idea of using sound "good" and rewarding. The drama cycle is running the show as the desire to use a substance increases. Stepping out of drama's relentless cycle is how we recover from dysfunctional habits and become the commander of our destiny.

Transcending Drama

The cycle of drama does not end. It's a merry-go-round that has no off-switch. People have tried to find the "right" meanings to manifest eternal happiness for eons. Others have attempted to remove all wanting from their life. Some try to control their emotions by being positive and finding the silver lining in events. Such practices interact with the drama cycle but do not bring it to an end. Freedom from drama is not achieved by changing or ending the cycle. Freedom arrives through transcendence. To transcend means to rise above. When we rise above the cycle of drama, we view our interactions with the world from a grander perspective. We take flight and soar as both eagle and condor in the sky of our consciousness. From a greater height we obtain freedom to select how we wish to interact with the world.

Nadine's story of her lost dog contains two characters interacting differently with the unfolding drama. Nadine was lost in her drama. She was a victim of her mind. Everyone who believed Nadine's story joined her in drama and felt the emotions of grief. They didn't accept the truth that no one knew the fate of Nadine's puppy. I listened to the stories. I watched grief consume the center. I did not participate in the drama. I stood in the place of "not-knowing". I observed and felt the suffering and witnessed energy being used to create sadness. I was outside the drama that enveloped the center while it surrounded everyone around me. Nadine was trapped in drama. I had transcended the drama of Nadine's lost dog. Our personal drama requires greater skills to transcend than the drama we see in others. Drama is transcended by remaining present while temptations to engage in drama entice us.

To an outside observer transcending drama may appear as a passive uncaring act. However, it is a very focused empathic activity. Transcending drama requires active nonparticipation while receiving intense sensations. We passively observe and feel while we actively decline involvement in drama. We focus on not participating in the elements that make up the drama cycle. The skills developed while learning the awareness principle allow us to use our wakefulness to light our path. For example, with awareness we focus our intent on not playing old roles or reacting to situations. We decline invitations to join drama and remain mindful of all we're experiencing. As we practice, we grow our access to presence.

Presence is a state of high awareness, alertness and attentiveness. It's being present in the moment. Presence is felt and resides beyond thoughts and feelings. Presence transcends drama because it is a state of consciousness that exist beyond the mind-based sense of self. Presence fuels the observer in us and sustains our ability to remain present. We give our presence to others when we turn our attention away from ourselves and toward them. Pure presence is existence with consciousness in communion with Life where Spirit, Body and Mind are harmoniously balanced.

Drama is Not Natural

Nature does not exhibit drama. Animals in the wild express conflicts but we don't see evidence that drama directs their life. Animals have wants, they take action and either get what they want or not. They accept their situation as a harmonious expression of life. They move on without demonstrating signs of drama. Natural order is expressed by balance and symbiotic relatedness that nurtures the continuity of all Life.

In contrast, our human world is filled with drama. We have drama in our personal lives and it's on display throughout our society. War is drama performed on a grand scale with destructive consequences. The condition of our planet is a manifestation of our unconscious addiction to drama.

Drama is not natural. So participation in drama is dissonant with natural order. Our mind is a storyteller and will continue to function whether or not it is in alignment with Nature. However, if our heart looses alignment with Life we will die. Our heart carries an inner knowing of what is required for the continuity of Life. The heart pumps Life's rhythm and keeps the beat of the body. The heart is our connection to health and wellbeing. The heart resonates with Nature's rhythms. As long as our heart is beating, it will lead us to harmony with Nature.

Finding balance between the heart and mind is developing harmony between condor and eagle in each of us. Eagle represents our mind. It loves thinking and believing it knows what's going on. Eagle represents power and control. The mind admires knowledge and seeks to understand. Striving for answers is a primary function of the mind. As presence emerges, our mind learns to listen to our heart; the sacred condor in us. We let go of our desire to find answers and welcome blessed inquiry.

Most practices for developing presence involve placing our attention into our body. Relaxation processes, yoga techniques and meditation ask us to focus on sensations of the body and cease participation in thinking. A sense of communion with life's splendor emerges as our mind becomes still. This is our condor taking flight. We open ourselves to greater possibilities. Our sensory perception increases as our condor soars. Awareness expands to include more than mental activities. We open ourselves to receive messages through the vast web of life. We leave the condition of our mind seeking answers and enter a state of wonder.

Return to your source of life when you're stuck in drama; with your mind racing, seeking answers to find happiness. Commune with the consciousness you share with everything. You're granted access to wisdom and insight through communion. You become alert and fully present like the lion, gazelle, bumble bee and crow when you connect with the web of life. Presence is what allows you to transcend drama and all the emotions of unhappiness. Learning how to do this requires discipline and practice.

Preparing for Presence - Stilling the Mind

It's no coincidence that most techniques for quieting the mind and summoning presence use the body as a doorway. Meditation, yoga and mindfulness practice direct us to place our attention on the sensations experienced by the body. Even shamanic drum journeys use the beat of a drum to resonate with the heartbeat of the universe. The body is our corridor; connecting us to the essence of Life; the Nature within us all.

There are many teachings and techniques to guide us to stillness and awaken our presence. The ability to become present and maintain presence is a skill that develops with practice. Here are a few techniques I have used and find valuable.

After returning from the hospital I had a taste of what was possible but I did not have the skill to remain present; in the current moment. Sleep was difficult for me. My mind was a marathon runner: processing, evaluating and judging. Continuous mental activity made lying in bed exhausting. Medication may have helped but I wanted a way to sleep that was natural and not induced by drugs. I instinctively knew somehow that my body would guide me. I needed a way to listen to my body to help me sleep. So I used a stethoscope to listen to my heart. I would lie in bed listening to "LUB-DUB—LUB-DUB—LUB-DUB" and it was exquisite. All that existed was the sound of my heart. I felt my chest rise and fall with each breath and the amazing beat of my echoing heart, "LUB-DUB—LUB-DUB—LUB-DUB". The experience brought me back to my mother's womb. It was hypnotic. I find biofeedback techniques very effective at silencing the mind and nurturing presence.

I discovered another method after a friend gifted me a small Native American drum. I used the drum to mimic my heartbeat. As I drummed; my attention aligned with the drum, my body and heart. I created communion between mind, body and spirit using a drum as an instrument. I continue to drum, play flutes, sing, dance, meditate, walk and commune with nature. My mind always goes quiet when I return my attention to Nature in observant ways.

I use many techniques to quiet my mind. During the day when I become aware of disharmonious mental activity or if I notice emotional distress, I take a few long deep diaphragm breaths and place all my attention into my hand. I ask myself, "Can I feel the life in my hand? What does it feel like?" I focus until I sense the tingly vibration that's like a hum. I dwell in the sensation that I call feeling of hand. Then I expand my awareness to the sensations of other parts of my body. My mind goes quiet when I journey in my body.

There are many methods available to help develop presence. I encourage you to discover and practice whatever approaches guide you toward spiritual communion with Life.

Blessed Inquiry with Emotional Guidance

Blessed inquiry is living with many questions. We ponder, "I wonder what is over the horizon?" When we live in inquiry, life is wonderful; as in, full of wonder. Blessed inquiry is a state of comfort with "not knowing". There is no drive to find the answer. There is no "need to know". The energy is calm and peaceful. Serenity remains ever-present with wonder as a constant comforting urge. Blessed inquiry is the explorer in us that seeks undiscovered places to go. The energy is dramatically different from the state of mind driven to find answers and a "need to know". Wanting answers and needing to know are often participants in a cycle of drama. Blessed inquiry is a state of consciousness unaffected by drama. Blessed inquiry is powerful presence pondering what is being experienced.

Living in inquiry is Nature's way. Animals, birds, fish and plants feel a sense of *"what's next?"* resonating through them as Life moves forward. A seed lingers in the soil, caressed in stillness through the cold darkness of winter. As warmth permeates the comforting soil and moisture kisses the seed. An urge to burst forth emerges. The urge is the feeling of *"what's next?"*. The seed pushes through its shell becoming a sprout. The sprout feels the same urge and grows roots, stems and leaves to become a plant. The song of *"what's next?"* is sung in all of nature. It is grounded in wonder and is the place of inquiry we share with all creation. Our drive to create and be authentic is the same force that moves the salmon to swim upstream no matter what. The root of blessed inquiry is this common urge that keeps Life moving on.

All Life exists in a continual state of blessed inquiry. Even our great Mother Earth wonders what we are becoming. She ponders how we will evolve. Mother contemplates all Life. Humans create and use inventions to control and dominate. She ponders, *"what's next?"* as natural habitat is destroyed; species decline and pollution flows in order to sustain commercial ventures. She asks, *"what's next?"* as chemicals are sprayed, killing plants, insects and animals. Mother accepts what is and wonders how to serve the continuity of Life. Nature feels Mother's urge, *"what's next?"* and new forms of life emerge. We call these new creations super-weeds, super-bugs and super-germs. They are Mother creating Life using our contribution to Life. Everything feels the urge *"what's next?"* as Life eats Life to create more Life.

The key to humanity's recovery for the individual and the collective is blessed inquiry with emotional guidance. For us to recovery we need to become present and feel the calling of *"what's next?"* within us. While in blessed inquiry we ask questions that help us see our state of alignment with the natural order of Life. We ponder such things as, "Are my desires supporting the continuity of Life or do they contribute to the destruction of Life? Does my reaction nurture relationship or does it create separation?" The counsel we seek during blessed inquiry is often found through emotional guidance.

In workshops, I use a metaphor of holding your breath to show how emotional guidance works. I lead the following meditation. "Place your attention on your breath. Breath in. Breath out. Focus on the transition of each breath. As you breath out the next breath, stop breathing in. Push all the air out of your lungs. Do not breathe in. Keep your lungs empty. ... Hold it ... Feel the force inside of you demanding you to breathe. ... Fight it ... Do not let air in. ... Feel the force; the calling insisting that you breathe. ... Hold your breath. ... Feel the force ... That force commanding you to breathe is your Life -force. It is the aliveness that is you asking you to listen, wake up and align with the continuity of Life."

In this exercise each participant is using their mind to dominate their lung's desire to breathe. Their mind is telling their lungs to go against Nature and stop supporting the continuity of Life. The mind is saying, "Hold your breath." Our Life-force resists. The lesson is that our mind may go against

Nature but our body will always align with the laws of Nature and seek to support the continuity of Life. Emotional guidance uses this fact to help us align our mind toward health and well-being.

Our emotions are like our lungs breathing harmoniously or gasping for air. When we are aligned with Life, we feel calm, peace, affection, attraction, acceptance, tenderness, compassion and love. Our emotions are breathing harmoniously with our mind. When we are out of balance with Life, we feel irritation, envy, disgust, fear, nervousness, resentment, worry and rage. Our emotions are gasping. We are "holding our breath". Our mind is out of alignment in some way and needs adjustment. Our emotions are expressions of our Life-force telling us to listen, wake-up, become present, adjust and align with Life. Our emotions are providing emotional guidance.

Drama is in the mind. It is not in the heart because the heart is in tune with Nature. Drama drives Condor from the sky of our consciousness. And without Condor we loose balance and harmony with the sacred, Nature and Life. When we find ourselves lost in drama our mind is dominated by some kind of power and control issues. Eagle has driven Condor from the sky. This is the time to still our mind, summon the presence of Condor and commune with the sacredness that is existence. Take flight with Condor. Glide on currents of compassionate divinity. Bond with love and purity. Then ask Condor such questions as, "Is my desire in harmony with Life? Can I accept this situation? Is the meaning I create supporting wellness? Is my emotion an expression of love?" If the answer is no, adjust and grow a new way of being with the situation. Follow Nature's way, accept what is and move on seeking to serve the continuity of Life.

Gratitude and Wanting

I used marijuana to quiet my mind through much of my adult life. Pot provided relief and shifted my perception. I became psychologically addicted. It was my support and medicine, helping me escape the wrath of my mind. After practicing the principles in this book and living in recovery for several years, I experienced a lovely illuminating moment. While driving to work, I quieted my mind by feeling the life energy of my hands grasping the steering wheel. The brisk air felt wonderfully refreshing. Highway rock formations gleamed, reflecting afternoon light and displayed a chorus of subtle colors. Trees were wondering if it's time to let the green fade and change color. The clear blue sky embraced the rolling hillside providing depth to the expansive forest greens. I was in awe of what I beheld. I felt the richness of existence. I remembered my days of drug use and noticed, *I'm high! I used to spend money for drugs so I could feel what I'm feeling right now! This is all natural and free! I'm truly blessed!*

Gratitude inspired me. I felt grateful for my life's journey, even with all the difficulties. I realized life was about weathering storms and growing through experience. It became evident to me that incredibly satisfying states of consciousness are obtainable without the use of drugs. It's possible to bloom like a flower using the astounding tool of gratefulness.

Nature connects all life through symbiotic relationships. Through relatedness the energy of life is guided. Gratitude and wanting share a symbiotic relationship. The wisdom of how they interact helps us manage our recovery.

A common question that points to the relation between gratitude and wanting is, "Do you see the glass half-empty or half-full?" When we feel ungrateful, thankless or unappreciative; our glass appears half-empty. There isn't enough. We feel limited, less than and feel a need for more. This is us in a state of wanting. Wanting nurtures sensations of limitation and lack. We perceive incompleteness. This frame of mind encourages separation and isolation. People express condemnation and blame. They may become abusive, rude and mean.

Gratitude creates a totally different experience. The glass is half-full from a perspective grounded in gratitude. When we're grateful; we express appreciation. We recognize and acknowledge. We praise and give thanks. Such expressions generate a loving and supportive frame of mind. When we're filled with gratitude, we appreciate what's in our life. Gratefulness nurtures connection and a feeling of abundance. We feel taken care of and a part of a greater whole. Gratitude supports the feeling of adequacy and sufficiency.

Being thankful is a portal to grander relatedness. Willingness to share comes easier. Gratitude brings light to dark emptiness. Gratitude fuels the flame of hope. In contrast, thanklessness is empty hollow darkness. It's a place of wanting that nurtures disdain and hopelessness. These two extremes are directly related through our consciousness. The more we feel one the less we feel the other. Greater gratitude lessens wanting. More wanting reduces gratefulness. Gratitude and wanting are attitudes that direct our connections and perceptions.

We can use gratitude to help improve awareness. Gratitude is like a set of corrective lenses, or contacts, for our mind. With gratitude we can see with greater clarity. Gratitude adjusts our perception in order to help guide our thoughts and emotions. Gratitude allows us to feel abundant and complete. We feel full. And willingness to share comes easier. Thoughts coming from being thankful are harmonious with abundance, sufficiency, appreciation and adequacy. These are energetic "emotions" that support the flow of universal kindness.

Through gratitude our minds align energetically to forces greater than ourselves. The 12th step of AA is a calling to express gratitude, "Having had a spiritual awakening as the result of these Steps, we tried to carry this message to alcoholics, and to practice these principles in all our affairs." The spiritual awakening that occurs is an alignment of consciousness to the sacred universal whole. Out of gratitude members seek to share their message. Gratitude is the attitude of being thankful. It's a powerful tool that supports recovery.

Gossip –Drama's Fuel Supply

When we gossip we're sharing reports about others. The information is generally not confirmed as being accurate. The juiciest and most tempting stories we share are the ones with the most meaning. An interesting quality of assigned meaning is that importance fades with time. We all have personal items that meant a great deal when we were young. Now their significance has faded. Over time, the attachments we create weaken. In order to sustain a level of importance, we need to agree that something still has value. Thus, meaning without agreement fades.

Erosion and decay happens to everything. Plants wither, tools rust and buildings deteriorate. The basic law of nature is that all forms are in transition. Our meanings and attachments obey the same principles. We paint houses to slow down weathering. Similarly, meaning is maintained by making agreements. Gossip is how we keep stories alive and full of energy. We invite others to believe our stories and if they agree to participate, the story lives on. When our rumor is personal and private, we spread gossip to ourself using voices in our head. We'll spin yarn and agree with stories we tell ourself about ourself. It's the basic maintenance required to keep stories alive in our mind. If we didn't gossip and seek agreements about what we feel is important, it would simply fade away and our attachments would disappear.

Agreements keep our assigned meaning alive and true. Without our participation, our attachments will dissolve naturally. We imprison the human spirit with our agreements of what we believe is "normal" or "real". Nadine agreed with herself that her dog was dying or dead. Others concurred. All who participated felt the emotional pain of a child dying. And it was all fueled by gossip.

I highly recommend active nonparticipation in gossip. Through the use of our awareness we can choose not to engage in drama with others and most importantly with ourself. It's amazing how many rumors a typical human spreads to themselves with the voices in their head. The drama cycle will run out of fuel without our contribution. Gossip is the fuel that keeps the system going. When we realize this, we can chose to say, "No thank you."

The Value of What We Are Not

The magnificent power of awareness provides the opportunity to see from a grander perspective. Human drama does serve a valuable purpose. It prepares us to see what is hard to see without contrast. The fundamental property of discernment is the ability to see differences. It's hard to see a white dot on white paper. And easy to see black on white. In order to see anything, we need to see what it is not. This contrast determines what we can discern. Artists often use the technique of looking at negative space to help present objects in their work. For example, a chair can be created by painting everything that is not the chair in the scene. In a similar way, human drama serves as the negative space on our journey to lightness of being.

When we examine our personal drama we discover there is something more—something not drama, yet full of aliveness in each of us. In this way, the drama in our life serves us by showing us, our unrealized potential.

I often use a blank piece of white paper to show the value of what many of us wish was not in our life. While I speak I fold the paper in half and begin ripping a small shape out of the paper's middle. I say something like, "Imagine all the problems in your life, the hardships and difficulties. Recall many of the notions and ideas you think about yourself, the judgments you make about yourself and others. Imagine all of it is represented by the white space on this paper. As we work to discover who and what we are, we see thought forms in our head that are this paper. All the things we think we are is not what we really are. Our perception is biased through our worldview. We consistently look at forms and believe life only exists in form. We've forgotten how to see and be with the formless. When we become aware and let go of our identification with things, our perception of form actually helps us see the formless dimension."

I show the paper that now has a whole in the shape of the star. I continue, "We are formless life energy in a physical body. The star represents our true formless essence; the white paper represents our perception of form. Our awareness of form allows us to see what we cannot see because it's formless.

The paper (form) allows us to see our true essence (formless). By seeing what we are not, we discover what we truly are. We are divine life force in a body, with a mind. Most are pretending to be something they are not. When we see our false sense of self, we recognize our true self. "

Our journey to light continues. The ability to expand awareness and discover our true essence is a magnificent blessings. We enter this world with innocence and a wonderful sense of adventure. What's amazing is how that original way of being is with us every moment. We're always here.

Transcending drama and returning to our authentic self is the grandest discovery possible. Many have said that drama is what makes us human. I say drama is what hinders our incredible potential. Those who think drama is normal and necessary have not experienced the bliss, joy, fulfillment and incredible peace that surrounds every moment.

Once I felt the space of a drama-free experience, I was not interested in returning to the vicious drama cycle. Why return to a place that limits and hinders my passions and self-expression? Why bind myself with agreements that restrict the flow of life force energy? Why leave heaven when it is here to play in? Those who speak as if drama is the spice of life have not tasted the incredible nectar of divine bliss and joy of being. Drama simply gets in the way of full expression of life, passion and love.

As we discover habits that are not serving our growth and development, we're presented with choice. With choice comes opportunity to change and look at things with fresh eyes. New perspectives begin to manifest in us as we practice taking care of our well-being and become aware of what serves us. We recognize what hinders our new way of living. Awareness lights the path and illuminates forks in the road. Recovery is about moving from old, habitual, non-supportive patterns toward healthy, nurturing growing practices. Recovery is letting go of old and making room for new. We identify what no longer serves then choose to nurture new growth. Realizing what is not working is a very important foundation in preparation for change.

Change is Transformation

Aligning our life with the principle, Presence Transcends Drama, leads to the mastery of transformation. I repeatedly hear the phrase, "change is hard", from behavioral health professionals. At times I wonder, "How many comprehend what they're saying?" The truth is, resistance to change is much harder than actual change. It takes more energy to resist and try to keep things the same. Change is very natural. It's seen everywhere. We call it growth.

Each year a tree grows new buds, branches and leaves. In the fall the leaves change as the tree shows its true colors. It rests during the winter months and resumes growing each spring. When does a tree stop changing? When does it say, "I'm done.

Now I'm a successful tree. I've made it!" It doesn't resist change, it grows on. The process of life is change. When we align with our life force change becomes simply our next step in a natural process.

Imagine a world where our conversation shifted from the illusion that "change is hard" to "change is the natural expression of life". What if we embraced the natural calling to transform and nurtured our continual evolution? Envision a world were we respect and honor the power of our consciousness. We are amazing divine creations sharing a world and universe with a vast collection of spiritual beings in infinite diverse forms. Discovering how to experience this reality is the eventual outcome from applying the Eagle Condor Principles.

Shining Light on Your Personal Drama

Awareness is required for us to see the drama in our life. We need to shine a light to help us see the shadows in our consciousness that keep the cycle of drama alive. Creating a record of drama cycle elements helps reveal shadows. You are encouraged to examine all of the items of the drama cycle to help you create your own personal inventory.

Examine Your Wants

Begin this process by freely expressing what you want. List everything you desire. Don't judge anything. Just write it down, record everything. List all the things you want. Let items arise. Express it all. Place no limitations, let it flow and place it on paper. Allow yourself to see all your wants and desires.

Reexamine your wants

We have authentic desires that are our inner flame seeking to express itself. There are also many wants and needs we agree we "should" have. These are conditioned desires, things we think we "should" have to make us happy, successful and accepted. Look at your list and see if you can identify the things you "should" want.

How can you tell the difference between authentic and conditioned desires? What happens when you consider letting go of your conditioned desires? Notice if meanings are revealed.

Judgments, Attachments & Meanings

How we interact with the world is often connected to the attachments and meanings we have assigned to what we see, observe and experience. In this exercise it's important to freely express what you believe is true. Be honest.

Here are some examples of how to play in this inquiry. Complete the following phrases.

I believe that a woman should … I believe a man should …

Fill pages with your beliefs. I believe that …

Complete the following statements.

I was told I should be …   I believe I am …

I believe others think I am …   I wish I could …

Examine the roles you play

There are many roles we have learned to play in order to make our way through the world. Many indigenous cultures use masks to symbolize our roles. We put on masks to fit in and be accepted. Some masks limit our self expression. Others give a sense of self importance. Think of the masks you put on and the roles you play. Here are some questions to help you get started and increase your awareness skill.

What roles do I play around others? I wear these masks because ...

What would happen if I didn't play this role?

What would happen if I authentically expressed myself?

Become the Silent Watcher

The way we transcend drama is by actively not participating in it while we allow it to play out. When you sense an experience of unease or unhappiness beginning to show up in you, see if you can watch the process play out. Simply be the silent watcher while you witness yourself judge a situation undesirable and generate emotions related to the event. Notice your mind recalling the rules and judgments that justify the unhappiness that is happening in the moment.

This is an advanced practice. It's Ok to get lost in drama and only be able to see through reflection; after the event. Over time, as you practice, your awareness will move from reflecting on how you were in the past to observation of how you are in the present moment.

CHAPTER FOUR

The Light of Recovery

"I give you the light of Eärendil, our most beloved star.
May it be a light for you in dark places, when all
other lights go out."

Galadriel says to Frodo in Lord of the Rings:
Fellowship of the Ring
- J.R.R. Tolkien

The space has been prepared by everyone with shared intent to commune with the sacredness of life. The fire is lit and sacred ceremony begins. Shadows dance, playing in the darkness. A flickering glow highlights trees, shrubs and structures. Black, amber and streaks of yellow dash about the village common. Light and dark play peek-a-boo to sounds of crackle and pop. The fire is ready and the people have gathered. The tribe encircles the central fire absorbing every word spoken by elders. They gaze into enchanting flames as elders speak.

"Tonight we share the wisdom of Fire and ask for harmony with Great Spirit. Fire is one of the great chiefs. Each sacred element carries great wisdom. Water teaches us of our emotions. Air shows us how to still our mind by following our breath. Earth displays our relatedness to everything and shows us how to steward the continuity of life. These great chiefs are wise and share their wisdom with all who are willing to open themselves and listen. Tonight we join with Fire to receive wisdom."

"Fire is very powerful and is to be honored and held sacred. Fire is the chief of transition. Fire creates and destroys. Fire brings us light and warmth. This gives us comfort. But when Fire is used carelessly, Fire will burn more than we desire and leave us cold, dark and lonely. Fire can bring destruction. Therefore we treat Fire with dignity and respect. "

"Fire consumes matter while dancing its transition dance. Fire releases spirit from material form. When burned, wooden logs become light; crackling sounds, heat, smoke, ash and dancing flames. Fire consumes but also frees spirit and delivers intent to Great Spirit. Through Fire we share our prayers and receive great wisdom. Fire speaks to those who are spiritually open to receive. Gaze into the fire and see Fire twirl as transition explodes before you. Listen to the sounds, taste the cedar and sage in the air. Look and see visions that only you will see. Spirit dances there using light and shadow to deliver messages to you. Open yourself and receive light through communion with Fire."

"During the day Father Sun shines down upon us and bathes us in sacred Fire-Light. Night is the time when we can gaze deeply into Fire and feel communion with everything. Fire brings sunlight to the night. The light from Fire is the light of the stars. Science says the space between stars is empty. That is not so. The space between stars is filled with starlight. The light between the stars is Fire-Light. Science also says matter is made of tiny things called atoms. Your atoms are like little stars and the space between them is also filled with Fire-Light. Fire-Light is in everything and is everywhere. You are a glow with Fire-Light. We are Fire-Light."

"In each of you is Fire-Light and like this village fire, your Fire requires tending. We all work together to nurture and keep this communal fire burning. We treat Fire like we treat life. When Fire is small, we only feed kindling. When Fire's grown and ablaze, logs are given. We tend Fire through storms and keep embers burning. Sacred offerings of tobacco and sage are given. We treat Fire as a grandparent with dignity and respect. Fire is not left alone without companionship. Love and reverence is appreciated by all. The same is true for your flame. We each have Fire to tend. Your flame provides power and illumination. If tended well your Fire will provide comfort and light through times of darkness. If neglected your Fire may smolder and die. Untended Fire can erupt and destroy what you love and hold dear. It's important to learn how to tend your Fire. The wisdom gained serves you and all life."

"The keepers of our ways tell us that long ago all the people of Earth were one tribe; one people with common wisdom shared and accepted by all. Great Spirit sent us in four directions to learn the ways of being human as an animal on this planet. Each direction was assigned the stewardship of a sacred element. We were given Earth as our chief and given the task of holding the ways of the Earth sacred until the time comes for the tribes to reunite and share wisdom. The tribe of the east was given Air as their chief. To the south went Water and to the north was sent Fire. The time has come for the tribes to become one again. Fire is what allows us to create ways to join together and burn down the barriers keeping us apart. We honor and respect Fire and embrace what Fire makes possible."

"The sacred elements need stewarding tribes to sustain balance and continuity of life in our material world. This is why creator placed us here. We're here to steward Fire, Earth, Air and Water. Some of our brothers and sisters have forgotten our purpose. As a result; Water is poisoned, Air is polluted, Earth loses fertility and Fire creates devastation. Harmony will return to our world when our family remembers its duty. Until that time, we will tend this fire and keep the door open to the sacred. We will be the light that shines when all other lights go out. We will be the fire of hope during the darkest hours. Our faith and perseverance will keep the light burning through the darkness so our family can return to their charge as stewards for the continuity of life. We will keep this light of recovery burning to help our tribes reunite."

PRINCIPLE

Fire Requires Tending

"There is an electric fire in human nature tending to purify -
so that among these human creatures there is continually
some birth of new heroism. "

-John Keats

Recovery is discovering how to open our mind to new
possibilities. Recovery is burning old patterns that no longer
serve us. Recovery is a process of change that allows us to
improve our health and strive to reach our full potential. Our
journey so far has introduced two masteries for recovery;
Awareness and Transformation. Awareness allows us to see
what works and doesn't work. Transformation is action that
creates change in our life. It's time to explore the third
mastery, Intent.

The best way to grasp intent is to observe the world of energy
and notice how Life feeds Life to sustain and create more Life.
Life is the flow of energy. Life creates motion in the material
world and intent is the force that drives it all. We see intent
expressed everywhere in nature. Plants grow, seeking to find

the best location for sunshine, water and minerals. A plant's growth is nature's intent moving matter. The force driving everything is intent. Salmon must swim upstream to spawn. Squirrels gather nuts for winter. Beavers build dams creating ponds. Birds build nest for their young. Nature's intent moves life forward.

An eagle soars with intent. It observes rising air currents and captures lift with its wings. The eagle stalks from above, scanning the lake, studying fish movement. A fish sees a tempting insect basking in sunlight above. As the fish approaches its prey, eagle wings tilt altering coarse to align and time life with precision and balance. Descending with accuracy, the fish reaches the surface as talons pierce the water's edge, grasping a life form destined to nurture eagle — together they soar away to engage in transformation. Alignment of mutual intent is how nature guides the continuity of Life.

All three masteries are displayed in that short eagle story. Awareness of many forces are tuned into by eagle. Intent drives the eagle's action. Intent moves the fish to the surface for a floating insect morsel. Transformation plays out in the fish and eagle's course adjustments and at the end when fish-life transforms into eagle-life. Such interdependency is seen everywhere. It is also present between the three aspects of change; awareness, transformation and intent. Intent is guided with awareness. Transformation is fueled by intent. And awareness requires intent to focus. The three masteries serve each other in symbiotic relatedness. Life's consciousness displays vast, intricate, harmonious collaboration. Honoring and acknowledging such infinite interconnectedness is humbling. Realizing we are in a great web of interdependent relationships helps us understand that we are not alone. We share the fire of Life with everything.

Fire Tending Is Self-Love Practice

Tending a fire teaches us how to act to maintain the flow of energy. We stir and rake the coals as needed. We add wood to keep the fire burning at a desired level. The elders of the village shared that each of us is Fire-Light and we have a flame that is to be respected and tended. Taking care of ourselves is the practice of fire tending. Treating our Fire-Light with dignity and respect is self-love. Many of us suffer from poor self-esteem and demeaning self-opinions. Negative attitudes smolder our fire. It's hard to feel empowered when our flame is suffocating with only a few embers glowing. Seeking to nurture hope with a depressive mindset is like tending fire during a heavy rain. Living with runaway anxiety is like tending a campfire through strong gusty winds. Taking care of our Fire means we watch how our thoughts, feelings and emotions are related and impact our personal power.

For years I allowed my opinions of self to justify substance use and unhealthy habits. It's easier to do unhealthy acts when you don't think highly of yourself. Discovering that I was the caretaker of my Fire-Light allowed me to honestly see the disgust I felt toward myself. I saw deceit in my mind; hidden in shadows. My outward appearance was maintained so others wouldn't see the truth of what I thought of me. I concealed my dislike very well. I complained that the world "should be fair to me" but I wasn't treating myself fairly. I was my worst critic. I wanted the world to treat me differently than I treated myself. I blamed the world for my problems and hated myself. I didn't know; The world was reflecting back to me what I was doing to myself. I was the one creating all of my suffering. I had no idea I was using my Fire-Light to create intense suicidal unhappiness. My Fire was burning out of control and destroying what I love; my life.

The modern American culture promotes a negative self-opinion that other cultures don't share. It's common for Americans to lack self-love. There are numerous self-help books designed to help people learn how to love themselves. Those books exist because the American culture lacks a loving nurturing supportive orientation. People from other cultures have mentioned to me how strange it is not to love yourself. Not all Americans lack self-love, however it is very common in American society. I've shared the challenge of learning to love myself with others on my personal journey. I've met many Americans who lack self-love.

Let's see how you resonate with your opinion of you. Take a few deep breaths and still your mind. Express some negative opinions you have about yourself. Example; *My grey hair makes me look old.* Next state positive opinions about yourself. *I look young for my age.* For many Americans it feels more accurate and natural to say negative things. It's easier to express flaws than to praise ourselves. Self-love is not admired and promoted in current American society. Advertising reinforces this by highlighting our flaws with offers to "fix" them.

Learning to receive my love was difficult and required daily practice. First I noticed how much I judged and criticized myself. Then I decided to change the game and make it fair. I figured why not be balanced rather than biased toward negativity. Whenever I noticed a critical disrespectful thought, I'd stop and think of a positive optimistic thing about myself. If I thought; *That was so stupid of me to lock my keys in the car*; I would pause and silently say something like; *You're smart and your college transcripts show it.* Each time I caught myself being critical I would create a positive counterweight in an effort to treat myself in a balanced fair way.

I was surprised how "normal" it felt to say negative things and very "odd" to say something positive. It became obvious that my opinion of self was fueling depression. The practice of finding a positive for each negative helped me become aware that I was smothering my flame. At first it was hard to find positive things to tell myself. I persevered and created the balance I sought and a terrific insight emerged. I realized that self-talk is a dominant influence on the experience of life. I also discovered that the need to have an opinion about myself is not required to enjoy life. I found that it was easier to stop gossiping about myself than it was to monitor my self-talk and make sure it was balanced. What my mind thinks of me became unimportant. There's so much more to life than my opinion of me.

Faith and Hope are nurtured by the company we keep.

While working as a substance abuse counselor in a detox unit, one of my functions was to write helpful notes on white boards in patient's rooms. One day I wrote this message; "Faith and hope are nurtured by the company we keep." It's a deeply profound statement when contemplated. The term "company we keep" is much more than friends and acquaintances. It's the conversations we engage in, the movies we watch, the events we go to. The "company we keep" is the energy we interact with. Most importantly, it means the conversations we have with ourselves – the voices in our head. *Is my company nurturing my wellness? Are the voices in my head supporting my wellbeing? Is my company healthy?* These are valuable questions. The "company we keep" is the energy we swim in. It's the sea of our communion.

A support group I facilitated engaged in an inquiry about hope. We began with the standard question, "What gives you hope?" We expressed things like; stories of others working through similar struggles, knowing I'm not alone and knowledge of effective treatment programs. Our inquiry went deeper. Together we wondered; How does hope happen? How does hope emerge when you're in great darkness? How does hope come to be when we are stuck in dark despair? We lingered in not knowing. We felt that place of hopelessness wondering how does hope appear? Eventually a word emerged that touched us all, "connection".

Hope emerges through connection. It comes through our Fire-Light as we connect to the light between the stars. When we are in darkness we do not see light. Black smoke fills our mind preventing us from seeing and feeling the Fire-Light that connects us to everything. Then a connection happens. Maybe a word is spoken by a friend or a bird sings a song in a tree. Hope emerges through a connection of our light to universal light. Hope happens when we commune with the sacredness that is life. Hope appears when we allow ourselves to feel sacredness. Hope comes from the Fire-Light that is us and in everything. And it is the company we keep that nurtures Hope.

If Not Me, Who?

Tending our fire involves maintaining our flame. We are the steward of our fire. It's our personal job to care for our Fire-Light. This can be very difficult in today's commercialized society. Advertising consistently presents solutions to fix our flaws. Hidden in promises to bring happiness is the message that you are unhappy without the product or service being advertised. This makes sense to advertisers because happy, contented and satisfied people do not feel needy and neediness sells product and services. Commercial advertising delivers messages that impacts us energetically. "This beer will give you a great party. This pill will get you ready for romance." Such messages say we need something outside of us to bring happiness. They imply we are not whole and complete. Such notions do not support our Fire. We're encouraged to seek power outside of ourself rather than fortifying our wholeness and completeness.

I used substances to help me manage most of my life. During my using years, alcohol was the solution to most of my emotional problems. A few drinks and a joint helped me find the happiness I craved whenever I felt too much stress. Alcohol and drugs were my fire tenders. I had surrendered my fire tending duty to mind altering substances. I looked outside myself for escape from the feelings I didn't like. I never knew I was creating a habit of seeking a solution from outside myself. I was a hamster on a wheel of emotion, running, seeking to escape emotions I hated. I didn't know I was the one powering the wheel. I blamed the world for my unhappiness without a clue that I was the fire keeper; tending emotional suffering.

My recovery didn't begin until I owned my inner flame. Many in recovery understand the place where we say, "Enough is enough!" Then we start taking action toward change. For each of us on our journey there is a special moment when we embrace the stewardship of our life. It's the time when we accept fire tending as our duty. Tending our Fire-Light is taking responsibility for our personal power and owning all the consequences of our actions, thoughts and emotions. Fire tending is taking charge of our energy exchanges in profound and deeply significant ways. We then bring forth change in ourselves and the world. Fire tending is a gift for life.

We are all unique and special. This is why the flame is so very precious. Only you can watch over your fire. Only you can identify how it shall be expressed. Someone dear to me gave me a Native American flute when I was in the dark place where life has no value. I placed the flute on my hospital night stand with no desire to touch it. My only desire was to end my existence. I let go of suffering and felt a glimpse of inner peace during my moment in light. Then my mind began racing again. I picked up the flute and began to breathe into it. I played as a child would play. I explored sounds, notes and tunes. I didn't wish to learn with my mind. I wanted to simply let out what I felt through my flute. Thus began my journey with flute magic. My flute taught me how to let my heart sing. After years of suppressing passion, I began to listen to my heart and rediscover what I truly love. It is our passion that heals. It's our authentic desires that promote and nurture our wellbeing. Expressing your passion through action is how your flame grows.

Passion is Fire

Passion is the spark that ignites inspiration and creativity. Our Fire-Light vents through passion. The activities we adore are like a chimney flue. They are the outlet for our passions. The things we love to do rise out of us like hot air up a chimney. If a chimney flue is blocked, the fire smothers. If we stop doing what we love to do, our flame smolders. Our creative actions serve our fire like the chimney flue serves its fire.

An excited child approaches an adult with their latest artistic creation. The open hearted child listening with anticipation hears, "A tree is not blue, the sun is not green, and the sky is not red." Even though, the child saw and recorded a wonderful green sun shining on a beautiful blue tree beneath a glorious red sky, those representations are not accepted. Unfortunately similar stories happen every day and almost everyone can relate to the feelings of the child in such a situation. Modern society is inconsistent at supporting the diversity of human passions. It promotes conformity more than individuality. At an early age we begin to express our passions to conform to the rules of others. The natural desire for acceptance drives many to suppress their passion to feel accepted.

Nurturing your inner flame means remembering how to feel, honor and respect your rich authentic passion. We're perkier and lighter when we recall the sensation of love flowing through us. There's nothing more fulfilling than doing things we love. Children know this naturally. They love playing and enjoying life. Fire tending restores us to our original state of innocent desire; this time with wisdom. Practicing fire tending is like waking the sleeping child in us and asking; "What makes you smile? What do you love? How can I help you be what you want to be? How can I support you?"

Fire is Energy

Fire is the power source of our society. At the heart of all technology is Fire. Our vehicles for transportation contain combustion engines driven by Fire. All our electric devices use energy coming from Fire. Some say, "What about hydroelectric power? That's water power, not Fire." Water flows downstream and dams generate electricity by tapping into this downward flow of water. But what drives the flow of water? How does water get upstream to keep the water turbines turning? Snow and rain on mountains feed creeks and streams that deliver potential energy to hydroelectric dams. But how does river water return to the mountain tops as snow and rain? Our glorious Father Sun evaporates water from lakes and oceans to seed clouds with rain and snow. Father Sun moves water from the ocean to the mountain. Father Sun is the source of all our power. All our energy sources are Star-Light. Even oil is Star-Light; captured by our plant ancestors and hugged by Mother Earth over millions of years.

How we relate to energy displays the way we treat Fire. Many do not treat Fire with respect. We see the consequences of our disrespect every day. Climate change, environmental degradation and wars are some of the large scale effects. Cancer, diseases and destructive relationships are a few of the personal consequences. Fire-Light is everywhere and in everything. The way we treat the sacredness of life is reflected in the material world. Our modern society treats the energy of Earth like an ignorant, uncaring, disrespectful camper who throws trash onto a campfire and pollutes the campground. The condition of our planet reflects our lack of awareness and respect for the power of Fire. The elders and villagers continue to pray that we will remember our duty and be stewards of the sacredness of Fire.

The world is a mirror reflecting inner and outer truths for us to see. As a collective, humanity's ignorance of our sacred duty is causing great harm to all life on Earth. The same is true for each of us individually. Our lack of awareness and acknowledgement of the sacredness of Fire shows up as destructive use of personal energy. We use our sacred life force in ways that create disharmony and sustains suffering rather than supporting harmony and health. Tending Fire means paying attention to our use of sacred Fire-Light. We learn how to treat ourselves and others with dignity and respect through the practice of Fire tending. We learn how to direct our energy as an expression of what we truly honor, respect and hold dear. Fire tending teaches us how to take care of our precious life force energy.

I used my energy in many dysfunctional ways before I began recovery work. I'd create thoughts that justified and rationalized my dysfunctional drinking behavior. The voice in my head would say; *If I don't drink, I won't be able to calm down and I'll be even worse. Besides, my drinking isn't hurting anybody.* I collected numerous reasons and explanations to justify my addictive behaviors. I blamed the world and others for my difficulties. *If work wasn't so stressful, I wouldn't need to drink. If she would just do her part, things would be fine.* My blame-thrower was my favorite tool. It made me right and others wrong. Being right was the most important thing. It removed me from any responsibility. Every problem was caused by others. Eventually I realized I was neglecting my duty as Fire-keeper. This realization was a powerful and humbling experience. My focus shifted from protecting my "right" point of view to exploring new perspectives. My Fire-Light was freed when I let go of my need to be right. This act of personal transformation occurred when I acknowledged that I have Fire within and it's mine to tend. I'm the one responsible for my Fire and its expression. I chose to stop fueling righteousness with my Star-Light and continue my quest to master Fire tending.

We select our actions with wisdom when we accept we have an inner flame that requires care and attention. We choose actions that are healthy usage of our energy. We encourage thoughts like, *Going to the support group tonight will give me hope. Janet always raises my spirit when I feel down. That book David spoke of is something that will help me.* As we practice tending our fire, we're also aware of activities that contain disharmonious energy potential. A few examples are; *Sally isn't someone to be around at this time. Whenever I watch that show I feel more anxious. That article explains why I need to limit my soda drinking.* We may observe negative self talk and think, *I'm really saying nasty things about me to myself. I'm going to stop doing that when I notice it.*

Our emotions express our Fire. Tending Fire means taking care of our emotional energy output and input. Remember the broadcast studio analogy? Our intent is the energy that keeps the station broadcasting and receiving. The phrase, "Garbage in, garbage out" fits for how to watch the emotional energies that surround us. Hanging around pessimism grows pessimism. Optimism grows optimism. Paying attention to the feelings we are receiving helps us recognize what we are tuning into. Observing the emotions we are putting out help us see how we are using our valuable Fire-Light. If we're not nurturing our health, it's time to change the channel. We do this by shifting our conscious frequency with mindfulness and meditative practices. We choose to be in company that supports a sustainable way of living.

Master Fire tending is the practice of guiding the continuity of harmonious energy interactions. Emotions exists to help manage the continuous flow of life energy. They are our mind alignment meter and rumble strip; helping us to wake up and adjust our frequency toward harmony. Emotions are part of the guidance system nature has provided to help us steer our mind toward authenticity and sacredness. Our emotions allow us to read the smoke and flames of our Fire. Competent Fire tending harmonizes Spirit, Body and Mind.

Sacred Energy in Motion

I've been fortunate to learn from a variety of indigenous elders. I continue to study and learn of the real magic that exists in our universe. A common thread that is sewn through many indigenous teachings concerns the sacred energy of life. Some Lakota teachers use a wonderful phrase that helps us connect to the sacredness in everything. *Taku Wakan Skan Skan* means, "Something that is Sacred Energy in Perpetual Motion".[8] Sacred energy is the energy of life flowing. Elders teach us to pray and feed this sacred energy that is in motion everywhere. It is what we call upon and seek alignment with during times of need. Indigenous healers tell us that illness is the result of a blockage of this flow of sacred energy. Such teachings are shared in the concepts of "chi" used in acupuncture and the energy of "chakras". It's no coincidence that energy healers from separate areas on Earth have similar descriptions of sacred energy in motion. It's part of universal consciousness. Everything's connected.

Everything is spiritual with physical manifestation. Illness appears when the flow of sacred energy is obstructed or misaligned. Sacred energy becomes stuck and begins to act like a black hole; sucking life away. It's similar to cancer or a parasite. Instead of supporting sustainability, life is being destroyed. Depression, addictions, mental disorders and physical ailments are all signs of disharmony in *Taku Wakan Skan Skan*.

All forms of trauma are a source of misalignment with "Something that is Sacred Energy in Perpetual Motion". Both historical and personal traumatic events affect the flow of sacred energy and the results manifest in numerous forms. Shamanic practitioners use a practice called soul retrieval to restore the flow. Other practices call it recapitulation and psychology uses therapy in attempts to bring harmony between consciousness and the sacred energy of life. All are seeking to restore harmony between Spirit, Body and Mind. Nurturing the sacred Fire within and seeking balance with Life are common threads through all the methodologies.

The Andean principle of *Ayni* (eye-knee), is a practice of "sacred reciprocity". Ayni is a principle for living that acknowledges in everything we do that "we are all related". Indigenous cultures all over the world live with awareness and respect of interrelatedness. This way of life is shared in indigenous communities and is also expressed in the Christian concept, "do onto others as you would have them do onto you." It's an ethical principle based on sacred relationship between people and all life on Earth. Ayni is as close as humans can get to living with awareness of our symbiotic relationships. In the Andean cultures, every interaction with the world includes an offering prior to receiving a gift from the Earth. The cycle of giving and receiving is nurtured. Practicing Ayni is the act of maintaining sacred energy that is in perpetual motion. Living through Ayni sustains *Taku Wakan Skan Skan.*

Sacred energy in perpetual motion is a natural fundamental principle that has been respected by indigenous people for eons. Modern society doesn't act in reverence with the sacred flow of Life. We call our relations "natural resources" and consume them at a growing rate. We treat our relatives on Earth as if they're things to be used and discarded. Our industrialized culture does not acknowledge the relatedness and interconnectedness that is real and ever present. The state of the world is showing us that our actions are dangerous to all life. We're destructive because we've lost our connection to sacredness. We've separated ourselves from universal consciousness and have been teaching each other how to remain separate for many generations. The time has come to reverse this process and allow the sacred Condor to fly with Eagle.

Arkan Lushwala, a fellow New Mexican and shamanic practitioner spoke of humanity's dangerous personal power when he wrote, "To carry any kind of powerful weapon in our hands or in our minds without first having awakened the sacred fire in our hearts makes us dangerous people."[9] This is true of both the collective and the individual. When our faith is invested in dysfunctional beliefs, we carry dangerous weapons in our mind. The weapons in our mind have great power and can be used for destruction or creation. We misuse our sacred Fire when mind has dominion over heart. We act with compassion and harmony when mind serves the heart. Aligning mind to serve the heart is how peace arrives and is the task of recovery.

The word *Munay* (moon-eye) in the Andean language of Runasimi has vast spiritual meaning. The term points to the incredible spiritual power that flows through our heart. Munay threads through all the spiritual qualities of compassion, acceptance and natural loving kindness. Munay carries all this and much more. Munay is the spiritual energy and power of love. Munay has qualities similar to faith with the added quality of active energy of love. In his book, *The Time of the Black Jaguar*, Arkan Lushwala described it this way, "Munay is the immense power that lives in the human heart that allows us to act in favor of what we love and what we want.[10] You do not possess Munay, it cannot be possessed. Munay arrives like a hummingbird to a flower. Munay appears when nectar is present. Munay shows up through our connection to the web of life. Munay emerges when we open our heart like a flower inviting love to flow through us.

We prevent the arrival of Munay when we act in selfish and greedy ways. The energy we swim in is the soil that grows our attitude and flowers don't grow in unfertile soil. Without flowers there is no nectar and no arrival of hummingbirds. The same is true with Munay. Nurturing and caring for our Fire is gardening the flow of energy and preparing our garden for Munay to visit. Through Munay's presence, we grow collaboration, compassion, acceptance and forgiveness. Munay pollinates harmony in personal and collective consciousness. Munay is the will of our heart.

Acknowledging and honoring the flow of sacred energy brings

balance to Spirit, Body and Mind. Indigenous wisdom carries great healing potential. Anyi nurtures gratitude and helps us remember that everything is connected. Munay aligns our mind and heart; summoning compassionate understanding. Bringing traditional teachings into modern life is fulfilling the eagle condor prophecy. Our mind serves the will of our heart when the eagle and condor share the sky. It's time for us to join the elders at the village fire and share each others wisdom and reunite the tribes of humanity.

Faith Guides Intent

Intent is another way to describe sacred energy in perpetual motion. The sacred force that moves the universe is intent. Everything is in motion because of this force. Water flows with intent to follow the path of least resistance. Water runs downstream from mountain top to ocean bottom. Sun adds Fire to water so moisture can rise and fill the sky with clouds, rain and snow. This returns water to the mountain top to begin another downward journey. Intent moves everything. The cycle of water is the cycle of life and shows us intent moving matter. Life essence is formless like the vapor that gathers to form clouds. Our formless essence falls into form like rain or snow arriving on the mountain top. We then begin a journey we call life. We're guided downstream within a vast flow of collective intent. How we flow in the stream defines what we do while in human form. We arrive at the ocean at the end of our days in our body and return to the formless like water returning to the sky. This cycle repeats endlessly and includes everything in existence. The water cycle reflects the cycle of Life.

Our world of commerce also flows with intent. Marketing campaigns are designed to capture our attention and have us align with the goods and services being sold. Advertisers want us to believe that what they're selling will give us what we want; some form of happiness. They ask us to put our faith in what they offer and buy their product or service. Our consumer based society floods us with temptations to purchase the latest item that will bring a smile to our face. They encourage us to look outside ourselves for joy and happiness. Modern consumerism promotes the belief that something outside of us will make us happy.

Immediate gratification is the basic promise promoted by consumerism. The fundamental assumption shared by many trapped in the consumption addiction is; *the more I possess the greater happiness I will feel.* We want happiness and contentment so we accept such notions. Addicts and alcoholics are familiar with the feelings of seeking relief using a substances. They have faith that the substance will make problems go away. And the truth is, it sort of works. Relief appears during use. But it's only a short term escape with temporary happiness effects. We cannot find lasting happiness from outside; we create happiness within using our Fire-Light. Lasting inner peace and joy flows out; not in.

Substance users share the belief that using drugs helps us get through life. They share faith that using is not harmful; it's helpful and good. They support each other with the intent to obtain immediate gratification and relief. Contrast this with people living in recovery. People seeking to live a sober life share faith that not using today will support long term health and happiness. They share the intent to not use today. These two groups have very different objectives but the relationship between intent and faith is the same. Namely, intent follows where we place our faith. Intent sticks to faith like glue. We can use our faith to get quick temporary relief or we can place our faith in a longer journey with lasting benefits. Monitoring how we align our faith helps us make informed choices.

How we invest our faith directs energy and impacts all life. Our modern culture associates faith with a religious context. I am not speaking of faith as a belief system. I am using faith to describe how we use and assign our life force energy. We guide the alignment of our Fire-Light using faith. Think of faith as something that directs our intent. When we place faith in an idea, our intent aligns with the idea. For example; our intent to purchase that shiny new car grows when we place our faith in the idea that we will be happy driving it to work each day. We eat certain foods and avoid others when we place our faith in what we learn about nutrition. Every action we take is an expressions of our intent. And intent is guided by what we choose to believe.

Think of intent as the force that drives water downstream. Beliefs are the land that defines how water will flow. Our faith is what we use to create sandbars, rapids and river bends. We are like beavers adjusting the flow of life's intent to create a pond and home. All the sticks and mud we use to alter water's flow are our beliefs we create by assigning our faith to ideas. Beliefs define how intent will flow just like a beaver dam defines how water will flow. Our beliefs guide intent like land guides water on it's flow to the sea.

Another way of looking at intent is to think of it as a fuel supply that sustains our desire to be healthy and whole. The light of awareness must shine for us to see through the dark smoke in our mind. Light comes from a burning flame on our personal lamp of recovery. As the light shines, it burns fuel. If all the oil is used, the light will go out. What is the lamp oil that keeps the fire burning? When people attend support groups, the greatest value obtained from the meeting is the intent that is nurtured and shared. People feel strong intent not to use for another day after attending a support meeting. Group members reinforce each other and it's their faith to move forward through adversity that fills the lamp. Shared intent is a powerful force and it's what moves us forward. Our lamp of recovery is fueled by intent. It's important to learn how to keep your lamp filled. You learn by tending your Fire-Light.

Integrity

When what we say and what we do are consistent, we express integrity. Our fire burns brighter when thoughts and actions are harmonious. Acting inauthentic smothers our inner flame. Our minds can fool us. We may "think" we value something but find ourselves acting the opposite. For example, if we say we value honesty and then lie. Do we really value honesty? What is it we do value? The answer is, we value something more than honesty. We choose what's most valuable in each moment. So it's important to watch what we say and what we do. The key is to observe our actions and maintain awareness of what we tell ourselves and others. Integrity nurtures our flame, dishonesty chokes it.

Fear is the fire that consumes everything it touches. Love is the fire that nurtures and sustains life. As you learn to tend your Fire-Light; reflect, remain alert, and learn to identify what fire you are tending. Are you nurturing fear or love? Fear has an energy that is different than love. Intent that flows through fear destroys. Intent that flows through love creates. Learning to feel the difference changes your life.[11]

Integrity is intent flowing through life with consistency.

Service Opens the Door to Self-love

I recommend finding ways to serve others. For many who begin walking a path of recovery, loving oneself isn't an easy task. Old habits suppress inner love. Serving others begins the reversal of this suppression. We tap into our fundamental life energy that is love in its purest form through service to others. It's no accident when we feel good and more alive simply by providing assistance to another. Acting in service to others helps nurture our inner flame. We feel a sense of love that is the essence of our true nature. Service is a gateway. It opens the door to our feelings and passions.

Practicing the Fire principle requires listening to your inner self that has been taught to remain quiet. Remembering what we love is not easy for many of us. Writing in a journal helps you remember passions. Think of activities you do where you lose the sense of time and simply love the moment. When you are in love with what you are doing, you are expressing life through your inner flame. Hiking, gardening, knitting, scrapbooking, singing, playing an instrument, cooking, creating art, dancing and many more activities can be expressions of the inner flame. Often the same activity can be uplifting and empowering for one or be confining, limiting and disempowering for another. What's important is your relationship with the action. How are you with the activity? Are you easily drawn into the moment? Do you feel a strong sense of aliveness as you participate? Are you honoring your wellness and partaking in life?

<u>No is Not a Dirty Word.</u>

Remember, *"Faith and hope are nurtured by the company we keep."* When I began my journey to wellness, I saw how parts of my life were not supporting my health. I made a conscious choice to walk away from some people. The teachings of the Toltec and don Miguel Ruiz speak of the rule of the Nagual (pronounced Ná wal). The rule states to always take care of the true authentic self. It means to love oneself first. Love yourself to overflowing, until love spills over and is felt by others. Often mastering this rule means learning to say "no"; not in a negative nasty way, but in an honest authentic way. Many people say "yes" out of fear of hurting another. This is a violation of the rule to be true to the authentic self. Being true to ourselves is how we tend and nurture our inner flame and make it stronger and brighter.

The way of the roadrunner as observed in nature teaches us how to tend our fire and be with our mind. Roadrunners have a clownish gait when walking and running. This is a reminder to us to not take ourselves to seriously. Roadrunners are fast and can run up to 17 miles per hour. They are very vocal and create a variety of sounds; chuckles, crows, clacking and coos. Roadrunner shows us to use energy (speed and sound) wisely. Roadrunners eat snakes and in the spring the male will catch a snake and eat half and then offer the rest to the female. The teaching from roadrunner is that it is important to honor your personal needs first before giving to others. This is not an act of selfishness, it is an expression of the value of balance and is often seen in nature. Roadrunner reminds us that attentiveness, effective action and the wise usage of energy supports balance and harmony.

Inside each of us, within our walls of belief and worldview, is Fire-Light. We are the stewards of our Fire. Our flame is our authentic truth, the essence of our life force. It is unique and precious. My journey to light requires I tend my fire with love while I question the foundation of my old beliefs. Other principles guide me in observing and managing a new harmonious worldview. The Fire tending principle is vital for it controls the flow the sacred energy required for all transformational work in recovery. Learning to take care of our Fire and maintain our desire to be well requires patience, practice and perseverance. We diligently observe how we interact with the world and with ourselves and nurture wisdom for health.

Pay attention to what you do and how you are being with what you do. Learn to see how you use your energy to create beliefs about things. See how some activities nurture your inner flame. Take note of the activities that limit and smother your Fire. Remember to observe your personal thoughts as well. Your thoughts are companions who are always with you. Is the company you keep guiding you to happiness or discomfort? If your company is not supporting your wellness, it is time create change. Often this means changing how you look at life.

The recovery road is unique to the individual. Each day is precious with new discoveries. We are always traveling and learning from our adventures. Sometimes we venture off into uncomfortable scary waters with a sense of foreboding. If we remember to tend our Fire and nurture our wellness, the waters become still. In the stillness and calm we can reflect and see how troubles and challenges serve us. Like the willow tree whose roots become stronger from bending with the wind, our trials strengthen us and guide us on our life's journey. We develop awareness of what matters and learn how we can make changes. The more we study, the more we see habits that formed during our innocence. With eagle sight, we alter perspectives; with condor feelings we embrace the sacred and transform how we experience life.

Here's some words of warning. Many who strive to be the authentic self choose to fight the domesticated self. Years of yoga training, years of meditative practice, years of disciplining the mind while the two selves do battle in an ongoing struggle for dominance of the life force they share. Days and weeks of inner peace appear only to fall victim to the evil ego once more. Such is the way of life for those who choose to fight the domesticated self.

Freedom from suffering, freedom from internal conflict can only be realized when we give up the fight and embrace "that which we are not" with love, compassion, humility and honesty. Only when we embrace and accept that which is not our authentic self can we become whole, complete and an ongoing natural expression of our divinity.

Tending fire is about watching how our Fire burns and how we are aligned with the sacredness of life. Each of us is alive. Each of us is sacred. As you pursue being your authentic self take care of how you choose to be with yourself. Tend your Fire with love.

We now have three principles that help us master the fundamental characteristics of consciousness: Awareness, Transformation and Intent. It's time to learn about the power of story and how intent is guided by the stories in our mind. We're on our way to becoming the creator of our authentic story. It's time to become an artist of a beautiful piece of art. We call the artwork, "life and the experience of being alive".

Fire Tending Exercises

Express your inner flame

Tending a fire involves helping it burn. The way we feed our fire is through expression of our passions. Suppressing our passions is like placing many green, wet branches onto a campfire. The fire underneath smolders seeking release. When our passions are freely expressed, our aliveness flows and richness emerges. Take a few moments and reflect on the following questions. *How do I express my passion. Does my love flow freely? Am I refrained from expressing my desires? What do I love? How do I express it? What are expressions of my passions?*

Practice Makes the Master

The work of don Miguel Ruiz; a great Toltec teacher, continue to guide me. It is the actions we take, the thoughts we manifest and energy we emote that are expressions of our intent. By observing and consciously choosing how we utilize our power, we realize our magnificent creative force. By acting and doing in a conscious manner we master our personal power. It is time to practice with reflection and observation.

Here are questions to help you get started on your journey of self discovery. As you complete these questions, contemplate new questions that will further your understanding of self and help you learn the power to recognize what guides you and what hinders you. The best questions are those you create for yourself.

Difficult times and significant events provide opportunity to change course. *What difficult times have I encountered that required I take a look at myself? What lessons did I realize as a result of the experience?*

What areas of my life support my well being?

What areas of my life are not supporting my well being?

What actions do I do that support my well being?

What "habitual ways" are not serving me at this time in my life?

Faith and Hope are Nurtured by the Company You Keep.

The company you keep is the energy you swim in. The energy can nurture your wellness or it can hinder recovery. It's important you learn to see how your environment interacts with your well being. Your company is both internal (self-talk) and external.

What company nurtures my desire to be authentic? (Internal and External)

What company limits my desire to be true to myself? (Internal & External)

141

Daily Reflection

It is important to develop the skill to observe the energy you both swim in and how energy flows through you. Without awareness, you cannot make choices and change toward what you really want. Whenever possible, ask yourself questions to learn more about what is going on within. Ask questions like;

How did I use my energy?

What unpleasant emotions am I feeling?

What actions/thoughts are leading to my feelings?

What do I believe is true related to my feelings?

What actions/thoughts can I create to change my reaction?

What can I hold to be true that will shift my perspective and support change?

CHAPTER FIVE

The Power of Story

"Those who do not have power over the story that dominates their lives, the power to retell it, rethink it, deconstruct it, joke about it, and change it as times change, truly are powerless, because they cannot think new thoughts."

-Salman Rushdie

I've shared three principles that I apply daily. I nurture my inner flame, maintain awareness and don't participate in drama. For example, when I awake, I give thanks for the many blessings bestowed upon me. After giving thanks: I ask myself how I shall maintain the precious light I carry. How will I express my aliveness this day? Am I present here in this moment? If I find myself acting out drama based on notions I think are true; I practice one of my activities to find stillness and inner peace. I may play my flute, take a mindful shower, meditate or practice deep breathing while journeying in my body. There are many activities possible and we each must find ways that work for us. Maybe walking, knitting or gardening nurture your wellness and help you feel alive. Some create music or write.

Taking care of our wellness and stepping out of drama is how we tend our flame and become brighter. While we do this, we are developing a sense of awareness. With awareness comes insight. With insight comes choice. With choice comes the opportunity to change from old ways that seem to run our life to new ways we create. We gradually move from habitual reaction patterns and emotional unrest to creative aliveness with inner peace.

Human drama is imagined reality. It can be unhealthy and extremely addictive. For generations we have been living in drama, teaching each other how to play specific roles. When we were young we pretended all the time and played great stories with our playmates. As we matured, we were told that our imaginings were not "real" and only the experiences shared by the majority of our culture are "real". What if all of us are still pretending; only as adults, we call our serious shared imaginings reality? What if it's all just a story that we agree to play together?

The way drama is remembered and shared is through story. It's how we allocate meaning and assert importance. History's filled with examples illustrating the power of story. Great orators have been able to move people to war and terrible acts through effective speech craft. Successful politicians and marketing executives are well versed in story presentation. A good story captures the source of our aliveness – our attention. When we surrender our attention to a story, we become captivated by it. We begin to live it, experience it and feel it as "real". When a story has our complete attention we become lost in it. When we're captured by story, our life force is used to promote the continuation of more story lines. We take on roles and use energy to act as playwrights have defined. Who are the playwrights? Each of us of course. We are the authors of our personal story.

My Role as Father

Playing father was a major influence that promoted self-doubt and persecution. I didn't wish to be like my father. I wanted to be the "perfect" dad but found myself a failure again and again. I also spent years playing the role of engineer and thinker. As I reflected on how I lived my life playing roles, I discovered my lack of presence to the current moment. I was often lost in my mind, thinking thoughts determined by the roles I played.

When my son was very young and learning baseball, I played catch with him on the lawn. I threw the ball in his direction and caught the ball when it returned. My presence was lost in a world of science and problem solving. My body was tossing a ball; yet my attention was not with my son and our activity. I was in my head working, being an engineer, trying to solve problems. Throughout my life, I missed many meals and family activities. My body was there but I wasn't present. When I saw how I was lost in thought, I saw how my presence had became lost in role playing and my life stories.

Stephen Hawking's Story

Stephen Hawking is a well known scientist and author. At the age of 21, while studying at University of Cambridge, he was diagnosed with amyotrophic lateral sclerosis. Doctors told him he should not expect to live more than two years. Mr. Hawking was given the opportunity to accept his doctor's story or create his own. His life is extraordinary. He is recognized around the world for his work in science. His spirit and mind are incredibly strong and he accepts his frail human body as he strives to express his passions. Stephen Hawking didn't accept his doctor's story. He chose to write his own. Mr. Hawking is an inspiration to all who are given a grim prognosis by medical professionals. The stories we create have incredible power.

Two Stories

The power of story is recognized by many in the behavioral health field. When learning Intentional Peer Support as developed by Shery Mead, we are asked to write our personal story from two different perspectives. One story describes our life from a perspective of a patient with symptoms and diagnosis. The other way to tell our story is from the perspective of life experiences with no clinical terminology; only events with feelings and emotions are used. We become familiar with the power of story while writing these stories. We see how our experience is influenced by how we perceive. And we learn that story influences our perception and our experience of life. [12]

I enjoyed the homework assignment of writing my personal story from two perspectives. It supported me in altering habitual ways of looking at life. What I thought was true turned out to be false. I stepped out of the my clinical story and new ways of experiencing life became possible. I began creating a new personal story and realized the power of storytelling. I discovered validation of ancient Toltec wisdom; we are dreamers dreaming stories all the time. The wise dream and don't believe their stories. The sleeping dreamers dream and believe their stories are "real". They live life in drama.

The Diagnosis Story

Change is in the air. People are reflecting, meditating and looking at life from different perspectives. The trend to awaken marches on. We still have a long way to go to free ourselves from our addiction to drama. In our attempt to help each other we can create imprisoning beliefs without realizing the consequences of our actions. I have participated in many support groups over the years. During AA meetings, people are encouraged to introduce themselves with a declaration such as, "Hi. My name's Gordon, and I'm an alcoholic." At first it was fine. I took it to be a declaration of truth that I give my power away to alcohol when I drink. As I progressed in recovery, something deep inside felt off when I said those words. It began to feel dishonest. I was labeling myself to be accepted. I was loosing my authenticity.

There is a strong effort in behavioral health to free people from the stigma that comes from seeking help. A diagnosis can be helpful or harmful. It depends on our level of awareness of how story impacts the experience of life. Am I an addict? Am I an alcoholic? Am I bipolar? Am I schizophrenic? The story of our diagnosis can be powerful drama. Some begin living life as the diagnosis defines them. Others find the descriptions in a diagnosis helpful in understanding their personal experiences. Their diagnosis is an answer that explains their symptoms. People find comfort from explanations.

Identifying oneself as an alcoholic or addict may help the individual understand their relationship to their drug of choice. Learning that symptoms are shared by others with the same diagnosis helps some realize that they are not alone. Knowing that others share symptoms is valuable. But, what is the value of labeling yourself or others as a diagnosis? How well does identification with a diagnosis serve after years of recovery work? Is it nurturing the evolution of consciousness? Or is it limiting the advancement to another level of awakening? What if we are not a diagnosis?

Sharing, acceptance, compassion and support can exist without labels. Strong efforts are being made by many to reduce the stigma associated with having a mental health diagnosis. Celebrities are speaking out and programs like Mental Health First Aid, are working to increase awareness of what life is like for those with a diagnosis. It's time to let labels fade away.

My Sick Story

I had an insightful experience concerning the power of story while working as an Intentional Peer Support Specialist in Maine. Cases of swine flu were being reported in the press. A fellow peer at the center called stating that medical professionals were running blood tests because she was suspected of having swine flu. A couple days later I shared with participants of my Toltec Wisdom Group, "One reason I'm feeling called to New Mexico is to learn about the energies of our mind and body. I want to discover how energy flows and how our minds interact with life force." Little did I know what my expression had summoned.

In the early evening I began feeling unsettled in my midsection. I recognized familiar sensations and realized I was sick and it felt like the flu. I began my healing sickness rituals. I swallowed numerous supplement pills and drank plenty of fluids. Worry grew in my mind. *What if I have swine flu? How will I get to my speaking engagement tomorrow? I can't drive a van full of people with the flu.* I went to bed and tried to sweat it out. I tossed and turned in a feverish state. I was in a sweat lodge; in my bed, under the covers. I shivered in freezing cold as my body burned. Then something came to me. A sense of clarity in my fog appeared. I realized I was playing a role of "being sick" like I had done most of my life. I recognized that I begin to "be sick" when I feel certain body sensations. I thought, *What if how I view these sensations is continuing a story that supports these feelings in my body? What if it's my story of "being sick" that I'm playing out here and now? What if I'm playing a role and my body is cooperating?*

I remembered my youth. My mother would shower me with attention when I felt sick. She served me hot soup and tucked me in bed. It felt grand to have so much attention. I felt loved and cared for during my "sick" times. I saw this as a story. Whenever I got symptoms like a runny nose or headache I would accept an explanation that involved a disease or virus. I believed the medical science description and my body played the roles. Memories flowed. I relived many episodes of sickness during my life while shivering with fever. I tossed and turned wishing the sensations would end and give me some peace. Through the burning skin, body aches and great discomfort, a message came to me. I felt a mysterious communication say, *"You've been given a gift and you're rejecting it. Shop rejecting and receive what has been given."* Lying in sweat; I wondered, *what does this mean?*

My old methods weren't working. I decided to try something new. I carried my blanket and pillow into the living room; turned on the television with no sound. This created a silvery flickering ambiance. I fluffed my pillow and caressed my body with a blanket. A ritual for this moment seemed like the thing to do. I took some relaxing breaths and began a meditative journey through my body. I started with my toes and scanned for sensations. I found hot uncomfortable areas in the ankles. I placed all my attention there; accepted my gift and held intent on transforming the sensation. To my amazement the feeling shifted from a burning hot ache to a gentle comforting hum. I moved my attention up my legs and through my body. Whenever I found an uncomfortable area I would hold my attention there; receive my gift, transform the sensation and move on. For about two hours I was in the recliner chair processing the gift given to me. I scanned, transformed and moved on. Eventually all the hot sensations were no more. There was nothing left to transform. I went to bed to sleep.

In the morning a miracle appeared to have happened. All my symptoms were gone. My body was fatigued but the flu sensations were gone. Since that day in the summer of 2009, I have not been "sick" again. I have walked away from my "sick story" and no longer play the role of victim of disease.

We Are Healers

We're powerful healers. We create stories and live each one with incredible resourcefulness. I'm not saying my story is truer than anyone else's. I simply know that the stories I create have great influence on my health and well-being. With awareness, I choose to craft stories that support, nurture and expand possibility rather than tales that limit, restrict and hinder my wellness. We are creators whether we acknowledge it or not. We direct amazing power. Our universe expands dramatically when we see the truth of our potential.

We can create stories that nurture and promote our wellness. Science calls what happens when we believe in something and it improves our health, the placebo effect. The term placebo is

Latin for "I will please". The effect is widely known. Science can't measure the forces and powers that manifest placebo effects but it is recognized as a real phenomenon. Placebo studies are done for medicines before approval. The placebo effect is physical evidence of the power of a story to support and nurture the physical body. Our consciousness directly impacts our healing potential. The placebo effect confirms this.

We also have the power to do ourselves harm with our consciousness. Some stories that we create promote harmful use of our energy. Resentment and bitterness toward another are maintained through the use of story. We sustain anger by repeating a narrative in our mind. When the power of story is used in a detrimental way, the physical body can manifest harmful, unpleasant and undesirable outcomes. Science uses the term nocebo (Latin: "I will harm") to describe this effect. It was termed by Walter Kennedy in 1961. Our mind has incredible power to influence responses in the body. Psychology Today reported that "when patients in double-blinded clinical trials are warned about the side effects they may experience if they're given the real drug, approximately 25% experience sometimes severe side effects, even when they're only taking sugar pills."[13]

The placebo and nocebo effects show us that the stories we believe influence our health. We can create stories that support life. Or we can create stories that inhibit the vitality of life. Our body listens to what we say even if we're unaware of what we're communicating. The effects of our storytelling do show up in the body. We can support our health by observing what we tell ourselves about everything we experience. It's important to develop awareness so we can pay attention to the stories we're creating in our conscious and unconscious mind.

The interrelatedness of our consciousness and body is complex with great mystery. Harnessing and using the mysterious forces that generate the placebo and nocebo effects is related to spiritual work. Shamanic, indigenous and faith healing practices help us to focus our attention toward harmony between Spirit-Body-Mind. Ceremony, prayer and meditation are a few examples of actions that tap into the mysterious universal healing potential that generates health. All activities that nurture feelings of gratitude and positive attitude support the placebo effect and produce healing benefits. Taking action to align our intent toward harmony and the continuity of life promotes wellness for ourself and others. Each of us is a healer for ourself and others. Universal interrelatedness says that as we heal ourself we heal the world. Seeking harmony and unification with the sacred returns us to balance that sustains all life. We become our healer.

The Movie of Life

Peter Russell presents a wonderful movie projector analogy that helps us understand our relationship to story in the documentary video "Primacy of Consciousness" [14] Great movies captivate us. We relate to characters and scenes and become involved as the story unfolds. Sensations and experiences manifest in us as we watch images on a screen with magnificent sound. We join in the movie. It feels like we're living with the movie. Such sensations come from our attention being totally given to the film. We live in the movie for an hour or so. It feels very real. We empathize and feel emotions with all that's presented.

We get caught up in what we perceive in the world the same way we get engrossed in a movie. We take on dramatic roles. We act and feel emotions like the actors we watch on the big screen. It all feels real. We get lost in our life story and everything we perceive. What if it's just a projection that we're experiencing? What if our life story isn't "real"? What if we're not defined by the story or events in our life?

A movie is a collection of images projected into a theater where people have experiences. The projector uses film to filter light and generate the images. Could we be the film that filters light to create images? This is partially true. The film in the projector is the framework for the images on the screen. Our worldview is similar. How we hold things effects what we perceive. Our collection of memories and beliefs are like the film in the projector. Over the course of our life we create our personal film that stablishes meaning and value to what we've learned. We carry our record of life in our worldview and it influences what we see and feel. So part of us is the film.

Changing your worldview is like changing film reels. Those working in recovery from alcohol and drugs are altering their relationship to substances. People with mental health diagnosis work to manage their symptoms in healthy ways. Anyone seeking to eat healthier food is shifting their point of view on what they eat. When we work to change our lifestyle we are adjusting our movie scenes, directing the lead character (us) and creating a new film. We get a new story by adjusting how we look at things. Changing the film in our projector creates different perceptions and alters life experiences. Part of us is the film but we are much more than a collection of past memories, beliefs and ideas.

The projector contains all the mechanisms that control the display of the movie. The projector determines the quality of the presentation of images and sound. Our mind performs the same function. It controls how we use our memories and beliefs. Our minds are like the projector and our knowledge is the movie film. We could say we are the projector. But that would be saying we are our minds. We are more than just our mind.

Stepped back even further, we notice that we're not the film or the projector that makes a movie. We're something more, something else entirely. The essence of what we are is the light that shines through the film and creates the movie. We are the light, the source of consciousness that brings forth perception. We are the light of creation. This is why we have the power to change the film and create new stories. We can change our perception and create new experiences. The essence of our consciousness is the light that brings forth the story. We are the creators, the playwrights of our story. Becoming aware of how we use our consciousness to manifest experience is the foundation for our journey to light.

Light is the source that creates all our experiences. A projector without light cannot project a movie. Film without light creates no image. If we were our story (the movie film) in the projector, we could never change. It wouldn't be possible to change our point of view. People see from new perspectives and we can change beliefs. We are light with creation power. The essence of what we are is pure light that shines through consciousness. We transform light to create the experience of each moment with our mind, memories and beliefs. It's all very magical. And the quest to grasp it all is an adventure.

Preparing for a New Story—Accepting Yourself

We don't leave the drama cycle by seeking to control outcomes. The desire to manipulate yourself or others is the seed that grows more drama. I spent years trying to fix myself in an effort to find happiness. I tried positive thinking and thought control. Such practices are helpful in developing awareness but they don't lead us out of drama. They do shift our attention and create a story based on self-focus and self-monitoring. When we're trying to "fix" ourselves we're reacting to an opinion that there's something wrong with us. We're attached to some meaning such as; *I'm sick, I'm evil, I'm a failure or I'm not good enough.* Inner peace, tranquility, serenity, harmony and bliss are not experienced when we're trying to "fix" ourselves. How could we feel such things when we're busy trying to repair our flaws? The desire to "fix" ourselves comes from a shadow in our mind. It's a form of self rejection. Accepting growth and supporting development generates change without the need to judge ourself as bad or inadequate. We can grow without feeling there is something wrong with us.

A plant grows and strives to expand. There's no evidence that it's criticizing itself and finding fault. Plants and animals move forward in life accepting what is and working with what is available. They seek to serve their life and the life that is everywhere. Asking how can I be of service for my advancement is a beautiful inquiry. It supports aliveness and aligns us with nature's flow. Life seeks to find ways to flourish. It's an instinctive calling. Everything resonates with the desire for continuity of life. Wondering how I can serve myself and others is the call of Nature within us. Contrast this with the story; *I must fix myself to stop causing pain and suffering.* Honest inquiry driven by the desire to see truth is more powerful than trying to fix a problem based on personal judgment from a story in our mind. Our stories greatly impact our desire to move forward. It's wise to create healthy ones.

It's easier to see things clearer when we come from a place of love and acceptance. You have grown to this point. You are reading these words because you have learned English and have advanced; developing many skills. You have grown and like a great redwood tree, you carry the wisdom of your life experiences with you at all times. The redwood ages and it also continues growing. We also age and continue to develop. Embracing our development from a service and continuity perspective empowers us and allows us to become inspirational storytellers.

Stories express our morals. What we believe is acceptable shapes how we narrate our personal story. Morals are our standards of measure that help us determine what to do. Unhealthy habits are examples of disharmony in our consciousness. We violate natural morals, often unconsciously, when we engage in activities that do harm to ourself or others. It's through the process of awakening that we come to see the truths that have been hidden in the shadows of our mind. We cultivate opportunities to transform by investigating our old story with love and acceptance. Seeing how the old story served us and "harmed" us provides us with wisdom that nurtures the growth of a new story.

Creating a New Story

Charles Dickens' classic, "A Christmas Carol", is a story of transformation. The spirit world sends messengers to the main character Ebenezer Scrooge to nurture his awakening and help him transcend his story of greed and selfishness. The ghost of his partner Jacob Marley appears bound in chains. The ghost says, "I wear the chain I forged in life. I made it link by link, and yard by yard ...". The spirit warns Ebenezer saying, "Or would you know, the weight and length of the strong coil you bear yourself? It was full as heavy and as long as this, seven Christmas Eves ago. You have labored on it since. It is a ponderous chain!" The symbolism is as relevant today as is was in Dickens' day. [15]

The links on the chains carried by Scrooge and Marley came from the attention they placed on greed. The chains became longer as they toiled for profit and remained unaware of their relationship with all life. We also create links on our personal chain when we assign meaning and attach ourself to our story. Our worldview is created link by link and yard by yard while we live in drama, unaware that we are a creative light force. The lock that holds our chain together and binds us is our belief in what we think we know. When we believe our story is the only way to perceive, we confine our point of view and limit our freedom. All locks have keys. And the key that unlocks our chain of attachments is the state of presence. We find the key through the mastery of awareness.

The Christmas Carol is a recovery story. Scrooge was addicted to greed. Spirits guided him through a night of inquiry where he observed his past, his present and future. Scrooge was shown his fate if he continued believing his story. Scrooge began Christmas Eve unaware he was suffering; locked in his worldview of self-centeredness, isolation and greed. In the course of a night he transcended his life story and became present to the connection we share with all life. He created a new story.

Great awakenings do occur but they have yet to become a common occurrence. My hospital experience was astounding. It showed me what exists and is possible. My old story returned but I was given a gift of insight. Spirit lit my fire of inquiry; driving me forward. I also had to embrace vulnerability and examine my worldview with scrutiny. I practice the principles in this book. I continue learning how to be the artist of my story. Recovery is the process called life. We're always growing; sprouting buds, extending branches and capturing light from different perspectives. We have more in common with trees than most are willing to admit.

Creating a new story requires awareness of our attention and energy. We master awareness, transformation and intent as we practice recovery principles. During the journey we learn; we're not the story of our life, we're not our worldview. We are the light of creation that allows us to create whatever perspective and story we desire. Paying attention to where we place our attention is a significant skill to develop. It allows us to see how our light energy is being used.

Personal energy follows attention. Our attention gets captured by a story when we're unaware. It's like getting lost in a movie. We play dramatic roles and react to situations. We feel our energy being drained when we're caught in drama. Stories need our personal energy to survive. We end up feeling exhausted after feeding dysfunctional stories. The less we participate in drama; the less energy we commit to role playing, the more energy we retain. More available energy means greater healing capacity and stronger potential for transformation.

Emotions are a wonderful indicator of how our energy is flowing. The feelings of anger, resentment, jealousy, envy and other forms of discontent have a different energetic sensation than those of contentment, peace, serenity, compassion and various forms of love. The energy of unhappiness is draining while the energy of love nurtures and sustains us. This is common sense knowledge that resides in our body. Everyone knows the difference between these feelings. But, we haven't been teaching each other how to

160

listen to this wisdom within. Our feelings are wonderful guides provided we understand how to use them for assistance.

The way to use your feelings for guidance is to explore the story behind what you are feeling at any given moment. Notice what you are experiencing. If you don't like what you're feeling, ask yourself, What's the story I'm telling myself that's unacceptable? Explore the story and then ask yourself, What story can I create about this that creates feelings I accept? When you ask yourself such questions, you're learning how to shift perspectives. You release attachment to your way of thinking about the situation.

Creating our story from an orientation of love requires awareness of our spirit, body and mind relationships. We can't be whole without harmony between them. Remember, everything is related and connected in an interwoven web of life. Some want to heal by focusing only on spirit. Others limit their attention to the body. And others choose the mind. A new healthy story contains balance of all three. Nature always works toward balance. We are wise to follow Nature's guidance.

I encourage you to create stories that nurture your well-being rather than stories that diminish your aliveness. As you do, you will find that the energy you use to create unhappiness becomes available for you to create joy. Get grounded in understanding that you're not the story you say you are. You're not your worldview. You are an amazing light force that shines and creates whatever perspective and story you desire. You are the creator of your experience. Embrace your creative power and become the artist of your life.

<u>Exercise: Examining Your Stories</u>

Perception Filters

Much of what we perceive is not original but seen through the eyes of experience. Our worldview plays like a movie as we experience life. It's a filter that influences how we interpret what we feel and see. It prevents us from seeing things originally. We see what we believe rather than seeing things fresh. Learning to see things anew has wonderful benefits. We react less and experience a greater richness of life.

Old ways of looking at life are like a pair of sunglasses that we are unaware we are wearing. Remember what it is like when you purchase a new pair of sunglasses. The first step is to realize you need a new pair of sunglasses. The next step is to pick out the style and color we like. Then we put them on. Then we take them off. We often repeat this process to see if we like the effect the glasses create. Learning to shift our perspective on life is similar to selecting sunglasses.

The first step is to realize what needs correction in our worldview. We do this by understanding and really seeing our worldview for what it is; a filter that taints our perception of life.

Use a journal and or notepad. Create as many descriptions as you can of how the world works. This creates a record of your worldview. Write explanations of why the world is as it is. This process removes your sunglasses and places them on the table.

Here are a few phrases to complete. Find at least three ways to complete each phrase. This is to help you get started. Often the best questions to answer are the ones that come to you. It is your inquiry. Each of us carries a calling inside to be authentic. We instinctively know what areas of life require our attention. Embrace inquiry. Get to know your worldview.

List the phrases you heard the most growing up.
List commonly held beliefs. Everybody knows that ...
What makes me angry is ...
What makes me sad is ...
What makes me frustrated is ...

Look at how you completed the phrases and ask yourself, "What are the underlying assumptions that sustain my point of view?"

Here are a couple examples:

Everyone knows that healthy people don't have my symptoms. — This assumes that I am not healthy because I have symptoms. It assumes my symptoms are unhealthy.

What makes me frustrated is how few people are waking up and seeing that their actions are hurting themselves and others. — This assumes things should be changing faster than they are. It assumes people shouldn't be unconscious and unaware of their environment. It assumes there is a "right" way for people to be that will fix the world.

What is your story about you?

The story we tell ourself defines how we feel about ourself. It is a powerful and personal expression of our life force. It shapes many of our actions and feelings. Many of our emotions come from the story we hold to be true about ourself. Some of it is unconscious without us knowing we carry unhealthy opinions about ourself. It can be challenging to uncover what we think about ourself. At first it may seem like vague sensations without actual thoughts. With practice we improve our awareness and learn how to express such feelings.

Write the story that defines you. Be honest and authentic. This is for you to see you in the light of truth and authenticity. What's your opinion of yourself? Who are you? How do you describe yourself? Express it all; The good, the bad and the ugly.

Explore New Perception

Share some times with things and explore new ways to be with the world. Use whatever senses call you. Maybe you wish to smell things in a new way. Maybe touch a familiar item with your eyes closed and discover something new. See if you can taste a flavor in a familiar food that you never noticed before. Feel the air on your skin or maybe feel sounds using your sense of touch. Explore your perception through all your sensory inputs. Discover fresh ways to experience. Return to your youthful exploring ways.

Record what you experience. Then share with others.

Changing Stories

Think of the last time you were upset. What were you feeling? Explore why you were feeling those feelings. What was the story? Write the events and all your reasons for feeling what you felt. List the assumptions that justify your feeling what you feel. Describe the rationale that substantiates your story. Provide as much detail as possible to explain why you were right to feel that way.

See if you can find another way to look at the situation. Can you find another point of view that nurtures and supports a different emotional response? Maybe pretending to be another player in the story shifts how you hold the situation. Explore a variety of ways to be in the same situation. Don't change the actual events that occurred. Keep everything the same only shift perspectives.

Perform a mindfulness exercise, meditate, breathe or walk in nature and manifest a place dominated by compassion, gratitude and acceptance. Then create a new story and way of being with the situation or topic. Change the narrative of the play. Shift how you choose to be with what's going on.

This exercise allows you to practice the first three principles and all your personal recovery techniques to start actively creating the dream of life that is your creation. The more this is practiced, the grandeur your life experience will become. Enjoy the journey.

CHAPTER SIX

The Child of Earth

A young girl of Earth is taught the ways of her culture. Innocently she embraces all she is shown as truth and believes it is the natural way. A guardian welcomes her to the land and shows her to her room. The room is a square cell with bars. The guardian removes a set of keys from the child's belt; opens the door and keeps the keys.

They enter the cell and the guardian explains, "The outside world is a very scary place. It is filled with great dangers. These walls are here to protect you and keep you safe from harm. Fear not for you are safe here."

The girl feels grateful and comforted by the warden's words. She asks, "I see how the walls protect me from the outside world. That helps me feel safe. But tell me, why are there bars and this locked door on the inside?"

The guardian explains, "There are others here who do not know you as I. They may wish to harm you. I know what is best for you. I will protect you. You are safe as long as I hold these keys."

The innocent child feels relieved knowing she will be safe from the dangers within and without. She trusts the warden's knowledge and experience. The warden locks the door and leaves.

The girl believes everything the warden says. She lives in her room and accepts all explanations the warden tells her about the world outside and the way things are inside this place. However, the girl longs to sing and dance, frolic and play.

The prison cell contains a flaw. It was constructed with a window that allows light to shine in. The window was a portal to the magical realm of possibility. Through the window the Child of Earth gazed and created wonderful imaginings. She dreamed of another world and another place. She allowed for possibilities the warden never spoke about. A seed of inquiry sprouted.

She pondered, "What are those keys the warden holds? Why does she hold them? Why can't I hold the keys and come and go as I please? What if what the warden says is not true?

Her journey began.

•••

Each of us is that child of Earth. We're taught the ways of our culture. We innocently accept what we're shown to be truths and believe it's the natural way. As our mind develops, our guardian arrives and helps us make sense of the world. We're told it's dangerous out in the world and we need boundaries to keep us safe.

Some readers of this book are female, others male. We each carry our personal guardian within. To honor both the masculine and feminine in each of us, I will refer to our guardian as both "him" and "her".

Our guardian provides comfort and gives us a sense that he's knowledgeable. We believe her and the knowledge she shares about who we are. Even though we want to remain safe and secure and accept what we're told, we also want to be free. In each of us is an ember of magic wanting to shine and sing with the stars. We sense there must be something more; that what we've been told may not be so. Our natural calling of authenticity summons inquiry. It's Nature in us asking, "What's Next?"

We become more confined by what we think we know as we accumulate knowledge and believe our guardian. The guardian becomes a warden; screening our interaction with the outside world. He judges everything and seeks to protect us. He claims to always be acting in our best interest. But remaining in control is really the warden's prime objective.

On that fateful day in the hospital I looked through the window of possibility. I felt a life that was free from my warden's control and domination. I wanted more and began my journey to light. Living the first three principles began a great shift, and eventually I learned to question what my warden said and try new approaches. What I experienced was a pendulum effect. I would feel calm and at peace with life and then find myself reacting, experiencing emotional distress. Then I would shift back to calmness for a period of time. This was followed by more reaction and a return to undesired states.

I was on a swing with stillness only happening for brief moments. I would find stillness and contentment, then slide down into unhappiness and discontent. Then I would rise up and find another brief moment of peace and calm. I couldn't find long lasting freedom from old habitual ways. I would recognize I was creating emotional discord then create inner peace and stillness for a while only to return to more dissatisfaction. I was caught in this endless cycle until I realized the fourth principle.

I embraced inquiry into the cause of this pattern. I saw that "what I believed" was creating my suffering. I recognized that the act of believing was imprisoning my true self. My warden was revealed and his trickery became apparent. I discovered the meaning of the walls, bars, window and keys. The light of inquiry exposed the warden and transformed our relationship. In the process, I discovered the nature of belief and faith.

PRINCIPLE

Belief Imprisons Spirit

"There is only one cause of unhappiness: the false beliefs you have in your head, beliefs so widespread, so commonly held, that it never occurs to you to question them."

-Anthony de Mello

The Child of Earth story is the tale of the domestication of our mind as we grow through innocent adolescence. The details of our life are unique but the symbols are common to everyone. Each of us is an Earth Child. The walls represent all the beliefs we hold about the outside world. These include our social and cultural values; our opinions of fame, fortune, social status and environmental issues. All of our beliefs involving the outside world are bricks in the wall. The bars of the Earth Child's cell signify our inner beliefs. Every idea, opinion and declaration we believe about ourself is a bar. The window to the world of possibility symbolizes our portal to the sacred. Through the window, our mind feels the magical sacredness of life. As we gaze out the window, our mind opens and communes with universal consciousness.

The guardian who becomes a warden is our inner protector, judge and punisher. He can also be the victim, perpetrator and rescuer. The guardian is the star performer acting whatever role we play. The movement from a guardian to warden represents a growing loss of presence as our mind becomes closed. We believe the warden's stories and let her have the keys. She controls us and we react; living in drama. Then the warden uses knowledge to explain what we do. We feel comfort with his reasons and explanation for our reactions. We are unaware we're in a cell, listening to a warden tell us stories of how it is. We have no idea she is holding our keys. That is, until we look out the window, start our inquiry and begin our journey to light.

Each moment of our life is a choice point. Every breath is a new beginning and a new opportunity. When we react and repeat unwanted habitual patterns, we're allowing our warden to control our life. We're acting, without conscious awareness, based on a worldview and history. We're failing to choose harmony with spirit and believing the knowledge of our warden. It's vital we learn how beliefs work and why we believe because the power of choice arrives with understanding the nature of believing.

Beliefs Manifest Consequences

Everything we believe generates consequences. People didn't sail far from shore when they believed the earth was flat. Their fear of falling over the edge prevented them from exploring. The belief that we're superior to others justifies slavery. As a result; people are treated like property, creating great human suffering and ongoing trauma. We believe low prices are a great idea as people suffer in laborious sweatshops to provide the lowest price. We purchase the latest fashion trend believing it will make us attractive while rivers are polluted with toxic chemicals to manufacture beautiful garments. The modern industrial way of life is believed to be the most satisfying as species go extinct and the climate of earth changes. Every day the condition of our world shows us the consequences of our beliefs.

At a personal level, every addict and alcoholic remembers the beliefs that began their journey to dependency, *This stuff is awesome. It gives me what I need - relief.* We become dependent on a preferred substance once we believe it is our best way to escape. Those with a mental health diagnosis may believe they are the story of their illness and live life as a patient, cripple or invalid - something flawed and unacceptable. People form opinions of themselves and believe such things as; *I'm unlikeable, I'm powerless, I'm not good enough. I'm a loser.* Such beliefs result in repeating dysfunctional patterns.

What we believe forms our worldview and filters what we perceive. This is why many of us seek to find the right things to believe to obtain happiness. A common phrase I often hear is, "I want to be with people who share my values. This is another version of, "I want to find like minded people who believe what I believe." These desires come from beliefs similar to, *If we all believe the same thing, then the world will work.* Humanity's been fighting over beliefs for eons. We're still doing it today. Has this approach been successful? Where has it led us?

We're at a great turning. Many are awakening. We're opening our consciousness to new possibilities. People are realizing that there are no "right" beliefs and finding the "right" belief doesn't create freedom. We've been asking erroneous questions and receiving incorrect answers. What you believe isn't nearly as important as comprehending how and why we believe. Such insight changes our world and provides perpetual freedom. We become masters of intent by understanding the process of believing. We recognize relationships between our beliefs and resulting consequences. Energy that was used in detrimental ways aligns to support the continuity of life. We direct our personal energy toward sustaining health and wellbeing for ourselves and toward a greater good.

Do I Believe or Do I Want to believe?

My workshops are often more guided inquiry than lectured instruction. I often ask participants, "How many of you believe you are the creator of your experience at any given moment?" In spiritual groups almost everyone raises their hand. I thank them and ask, "How many of you experience some level of anger, frustration, resentment, jealousy, discontent or any other feeling you don't want to have?" After many of the same hands rise, I continue, "Isn't that interesting. How can that be? If you are the creator of your experience why are you creating feelings you don't want? Do you miss suffering? Then decide; I haven't felt awful in so long, I need to feel terrible for awhile. Is that what you do? Why would you do something other than what you believe is true? Do you believe it or not? What's going on?"

It is possible to become the master creator of the experience you are having in the moment. However, wanting to believe something is different from believing it. Understanding the difference comes with experience and awareness of how, why and what we believe.

Belief and Believing

The American Heritage Dictionary defines belief as, "Something accepted as true." A belief is an idea, notion or concept we accept as true. Our minds are filled with ideas and concepts but not all are believed. We can think of: *a blue tree, purple banana, a talking duck or even a cow jumping over the moon.* We create infinite assortments of imaginings that we don't hold as truth. We also generate thoughts that we accept as true. For example: *the sky is blue. The grass is green. Ripe bananas are yellow.* These are shared beliefs of many. However, those who are color blind may not share these beliefs. It's important to note that what we categorize as true is rarely, if ever, true for everyone.

Beliefs are created through the act of believing. A teapot and cup analogy helps illustrate the relationship between a belief and believing. Imagine you hold a magic teapot. Before you on a vast table are cups as far as the eye can see. Each cup represents an idea, notion or concept such as; *cats meow, dogs bark, trees talk, dolphins walk, money is power, boundaries protect us, parents don't care, I'm not important* and so on. You are free to choose which cups to fill and which to leave empty. You can place as much tea as you want in whatever cup you desire. The act of believing is pouring tea into a cup. The more tea you pour into the cup, the stronger your belief. When a cup contains tea, it's a belief. If it's empty, you don't believe it's true. Beliefs are not permanent. For example, people used to believe *the world is flat*. Now we believe *the Earth is round*. When we let go of a belief we're pouring tea out of the cup. No tea in cup, no belief. And the act of pouring tea is believing.

Energy of Belief

When I ask, "How do you create a belief?" the most common reply is, "I believe something to be true." That really doesn't explain it. We need to go deeper. How do we make something true in our mind? What happens when we move an idea from an impartial thought into a belief? Think of the teapot. What is the tea that we pour into the cup?

To understand the tea we need to consider personal energy. Imagine a boy is working on a school project. He uses his father's favorite tool without asking permission. The boy has an accident and breaks the tool. He imagines his father's anger and believes he's going to be punished severely. His belief generates fear that bad stuff is going to happen. Dread and anxiety swell in him as he tries to hide his actions. He can't sleep at night; worrying about what his father will do when he finds out. He suffers in anguish waiting for his world to come to an end. His belief in what will transpire generates great torment.

Now imagine that dreadful moment. His father enters his room holding the broken tool in his hand. The boy's heart sinks into his stomach. Then his father smiles and says, "Johnny, I'm so proud of you! I saw your project. You did that all by yourself. What a great job! I'm very impressed!"

"But what about your tool? I know it was your favorite. I'm sorry. I didn't mean to break it," the boy replies.

"The tool's not as important as what you've accomplished. I'm so proud of you!" His father says while hugging him.

Imagine the experience of the little boy. Empathize with the great feeling of relief. Things didn't turn out as he feared. Relate this to an experience you had when you believed things were going to be dreadful and then everything turned out fine. Remember the sense of relief you felt. That sense of relief; that sensation of becoming lighter, the feeling of release is energy in motion. The energy that causes that feeling of relief is the magical element of beliefs. It's the magic tea we pour while believing.

Nadine's lost dog story displays the same energy exchanges. While she believed her beloved puppy was lying concealed in bushes dying, her cycle of drama consumed energy from all who participated. When she heard the news of her puppy's well -being, great relief was felt by everyone. A feeling of release of energy that is bound with fear is felt when a negative belief is released. We feel a sensation of energy flowing. Thus, the magic tea is a form of energy that can be felt when the cup is emptied. This is a valuable insight. We add energy to ideas to create beliefs. This energy is felt when we let go of a belief. What is this energy?

Creating a Belief

The root of a belief's energy exchange is identification or attachment. Relief arrives when we break our attachment with a belief. The attachment is created through the process of identification. When a man says, "I am male." He equates his sense of self with the meaning of the word male. He identifies with the idea, *male*. The words my and mine act the same way. Taking things personally is the act of identifying our sense of self with things. Believing this is; *my cat, my house, my job* are identifications of self with different forms. Identification is the process used to form attachments.

When we identify with an idea or concept, we become one with an impartial thought. We assign some of our precious life force energy to an idea and create a belief. The energy we attach is like glue and binds us to the thought; making us and the idea one and the same. When we let go of a belief, we feel a sensation of relief. What we are experiencing is light force returning to us and it feels pleasant and freeing. A lighter sense of being emerges. The lightness is the freeing of light energy. We feel such sensations as energy is released from a commitment and becomes free and available.

178

When we create a belief, we take a little piece of our life energy and bond it to a thought form and personalize it. Imagine ideas, notions and concepts as bricks. We take these bricks and add life energy to create beliefs. Our personal energy acts like mortar and binds the bricks together. We slowly create a wall of beliefs and explanations using our life energy to bond it together and hold it in place.

I use the words light and life to describe the energy that creates beliefs and bonds them. The light between the stars is the same light that is between the atoms in our body. Light fills the universe and connects everything. Light bonds the web of life together. Light energy is life energy. Science is beginning to recognize the mysterious qualities of light. Currently, spirituality is more aligned with light's relationship to belief and believing than science.

In the Child of the Earth story, the outer walls represent our beliefs about the outside world. The bricks are held in place with mortar composed of spirit energy, or light energy. The inside bars symbolize our personal beliefs about ourself. They're also held in place with our life energy. Welded bonds are strong and hard to break. The same is true of our deeply held personal beliefs. Here's another way to look at it. Our personal belief cups are larger and can hold more magic tea than the cups representing our beliefs about the world in general.

There's deep meaning within the Child of Earth tale. As the child grows, she is innocently building her room, brick by brick and bar by bar. She learns from her life and accepts the beliefs of others as her own. She forms opinions of herself that she believes are true. As we grow up, we are given many bricks by others. We hear, "It's important to get an education so you can be somebody. You need to compete and do better than others so you can succeed." And our innocent minds believe. We unknowingly fill our cups with the magic force that is our eternal light. We commit life essence into an evolving system of beliefs.

There are hidden messages in much of what we believe. Our worldview is the collection of all our beliefs. It includes ideas we knowingly accept and many that are hidden in shadow, away from the prying eye of our awareness. Each belief is a brick in the wall we assemble. We build it brick by brick, idea by idea, notion by notion, and it's held in place with our life force energy. Our worldview dominates our perception and generates the majority of our emotional pain and suffering. When what we believe is not in harmony with our authentic essence, we experience unhappiness in all its diversity. We manifest sadness, shame, self-pity, greed, guilt, inferiority, anger, resentment, false pride, superiority, ego and much more. These are the times when we're listening to our warden and believing lies in our worldview. Our body reacts with negative emotions signaling to us that we're out of alignment but we don't listen. We press on creating more suffering.

The energy we place into a belief is a special energy and can be felt. We feel it when we let go of beliefs. We're all aware of this phenomena at a fundamental level. This is evidenced in several common expressions; spiritual journeys are called paths to enlightenment. They're not "paths to darkness" or "roads to heaviness". When we help others through emotional distress, we encourage them to, "let go". We don't say "take on more burdens!" The commonly used term, "lighten up" inspires us to release our attachments. Instinctively we're aware that we're being asked to become lighter and embrace "the light".

Thousands of teachings are available and they all help us learn how to develop a state of communion with the power of Life that is greater than the singular, mind based, sense of self. Spiritual traditions allow us to experience the immeasurable and mysterious dimension of Life. This is vital for our understanding because the application of faith is learned directly through spiritual practice. And faith happens to be the magic tea we pour into our belief cups.

Faith

Describing faith is like seeking to describe love. It's a task of poets, an endless quest to place into form, magnificent indefinable formlessness. Words approximate but can't seem to capture it all. Here are a few beautiful attempts by others.

"Faith is the bird that feels the light when the dawn is still dark."

- Rabindranath Tagore

"Faith is permitting ourselves to be seized by the things we do not see."

- Martin Luther

"Faith is an oasis in the heart which will never be reached by the caravan of thinking."
- Khalil Gibran

Faith is the magic tea, the mortar that bonds our essence to thoughts in the mind. It guides interaction between consciousness and material manifestation. Faith is magical and flows through everything. We commune between the material and spiritual dimensions through our use of faith. It involves relationships and energetic exchanges. Faith is simple to apply yet complex to fathom with its infinite interrelatedness.

The pouring of our magic tea is the act of believing. As we pour we are investing our faith into the cup of our choosing. For example; if I believe *things make me happy.* That means I have poured my tea (faith) into the idea; *material possessions create happiness.* I have invested my faith into the notion; *the more I possess the happier I will feel.* Many people have made such a faith investment. The consequences of billions of people sharing this belief are; environmental decay, social injustice and spiritual emptiness. The power of our collective faith is astounding! The beliefs we share and our faith in those beliefs is the root source of most suffering. Our planet is changing; species are going extinct, ecosystems are in decay. And it all comes from our faith directing the transformation of life; without awareness. Someday we will realize the power of our faith and use it with wisdom to nurture and sustain the continuity of life.

It's unfortunate that many decline opportunities to explore the nature of faith and the bounty of harmony obtained through spiritual pursuits. It's OK. Faith doesn't care. Faith has no judgement. Nature's universal consciousness doesn't judge. Judgement is a human process that we learn during domestication as our personal guardian transforms into our warden keeping us in our trance. It's fine if you place your faith in science, religion, atheism or indigenous and new age spirituality. It doesn't matter. It's your choice. Each of us chooses where to place our faith. That is the glorious blessing of individuality that nurtures diversity and supports the grandeur of the whole.

Each of us stands before an expansive table with an infinite variety of cups before us. We are the ones with a magic teapot containing our faith. Awareness allows us to look at the cups and see how they lay on the table. Relationships between cups and our world can be seen. Maybe the table cloth has stains from spilled magic. Some cups may be cracked or broken. We choose what cups to fill and what cups to leave empty. We choose how to pour our tea. Faith is the one feature of life that is totally unique and ours to command. Others may tempt and ask us to place faith in their cups; but the ultimate choice is ours alone. We are choosers choosing how to assign our faith. We select what we will trust and what we refuse to believe. Freedom arrives through acceptance of this fundamental truth.

Faith is the playground where thoughts and feelings play with the unfolding of space and time. It's a place of natural divine communion. Life is the schoolyard. We all share this sacred area with astounding interrelatedness. All is playing together. Some play is pleasant; some play is nasty. When faith is used in punitive ways, everything feels the shards of rain in harsh wind. Rigid idealism is faith turned controlling and domineering. When faith is applied in beneficial ways, sun fills the yard with warmth and soft breezes bring pleasure. Adaptable acceptance is faith used democratically. We are playing in faith every moment of existence. Faith is the root system that connects everything and communicates intent through universal consciousness. We can guide our faith in ways that nurture and sustain life or we can direct our faith in ways that do harm to ourself and others. Awakening allows us to hold our teapot and pour our magic tea using wisdom to create harmony; both within and without.

<u>Opening the Sacred Window</u>

As the Child of Earth looked out the window she imagined new possibilities. She communed with universal consciousness and touched the sacredness of life. As a result, believing what the warden told her lost it's appeal. She moved from seeking answers from her captor to living in authentic inquiry. She changed the relationship she had with what she thought she knew. As she questioned her beliefs, she emptied cups and recovered her faith. This enlarged the window of her cell and increased her ability to experience the sacredness of all things.

People with rigid belief systems have their faith tightly bound in beliefs. They have limited free consciousness because continual investment of faith energy is required to keep a mind rigid and fixed. They need reasons, justifications and agreements to keep their worldview intact. It's hard to let go when you're constantly using energy to sustain your point of view. Closed minded people live with their warden dominating their perception. Their window of possibility is bricked up; covered with layers of beliefs. It's hard to find free energy to question what we think is true when our faith is committed to our belief system. However the evolution of consciousness goes on, even for the stubborn. Often life delivers a crashing blow creating a crack to let light in.

It's common for people to experience events that shatter their walls of belief. Many with substance abuse problems need to hit rock bottom before they are willing to question what they believe. I had my hospital experience. Others lose their job or family. Life works in mysterious ways to guide the evolution of consciousness. If we're unwilling to look at our dysfunction, the events in life will display our need to change in radiant color. It may not be pretty but it's universal guidance demanding that we awaken from our trance. The light of possibility shines into what may seem like chaos and wreckage. Such events are pivotal turning points for many because habitual disharmonious patterns are being highlighted. Those willing to awaken, grow and benefit from what feels like crisis.

We are connected in ways that are beyond our ability to comprehend. Earth is showing evidence of environmental crisis and humanity's state of consciousness is a causal factor.

Those suffering with addiction to drugs, alcohol, food, shopping, and greed are all a part of this great demonstration of collective dysfunction. A great shaking is occurring. A colossal wrecking ball is slamming into the prison walls of humanity's belief systems. Everyone is being asked to wake up and examine how we are investing our faith. Life is asking us to question what we believe and take the keys from the warden and create a world that is sustainable, just and honors the sacredness of Life.

Destructive Unconscious Beliefs

"The great lie is that it is civilization. It's not civilized. It has been literally the most blood thirsty brutalizing system ever imposed upon this planet. That is not civilization. That's the great lie, is that it represents civilization." - John Trudell

There are beliefs that nurture and support the continuity of life and there are beliefs that do quite the opposite. Humanity has been passing on dysfunctional beliefs for generations. Beliefs that support sustainability, honor and respect life have not been embraced. Beliefs that promote consumption and disrespect for nature are encouraged. Humanity continues to wage war on itself and Nature. The source of all the devastation comes from beliefs we unconsciously share. It has gotten to the point where all life on Earth is being harmed from unrecognized addictions and unexamined belief systems.

The indigenous people of the world are aware of the disharmonious state of mind that is shared in the modern industrialized world. The treaties broken in North America and the violated agreements with indigenous people around the globe are testimonies of the dominant destructive belief systems driving the modern consuming world. The need to have and use more arises from beliefs that are innocently passed on through generations. We're running out of Earth and experiencing the consequences of our dysfunctional lifestyles.

The Lakota of the great plains have a rich history and a strong determination to retain their culture. Their enduring strength has been demonstrated through years of poverty, disease and attempts to destroy their culture. They survive. When they first met the Europeans they noticed something odd about them. They used the term *Wasi'chu* to describe them. It means "non-Indian" but over time it has come to mean such things as "greedy", "takes the fat" and "takes the best for themselves". Wasi'chu is a state of mind that appears like a mental illness to those who do not share the same cultural beliefs. The Lakota do not share the belief of ownership as carried by most of the industrialized world. Like many indigenous people they believe the land owns them rather than humans owning the land. Crazy Horse said, "One does not sell the land people walk on." Such fundamental differences in beliefs have been the source of great suffering and turmoil.

Wasi'chu is a state of mind that is based on beliefs that support behaviors that go against the laws of Nature. It's an illness in the human consciousness and is shared through domestication and agreement. It hides in us without our awareness. It's an unrecognized addiction. When we suffer from Wasi'chu we whole-heartedly believe; with no doubt, that *it is beautiful and good to possess more than we need.* When we're infected with Wasi'chu we believe; *having things creates happiness, things are not alive, we're not related, we're separate from each other and other life forms, we're here to take and use what we need.* We measure our worth by how much we control and possess. Modern consumerism is based on these beliefs.

Johansen and Maestas wrote, "Wasi'chu is also a human condition based on inhumanity, racism, and exploitation. It is a sickness, a seemingly incurable and contagious disease which begot the ever advancing society of the West. If we do not control it, this disease will surely be the basis for what may be the last of the continuing wars against the Native American people." [16]

The great turning of climate, ecological systems and economic uncertainty are warnings that "rock-bottom" is approaching. Human consciousness filled with addictions is manifesting consequences on a planetary scale like an alcoholic or addict creates at a local level. Our beliefs are driving us to behave in patterns that are not sustainable and bring great suffering to life that shares this planet with us.

Mother Earth is calling us to awaken and recognize our dysfunctional beliefs and listen to the wisdom being shared by the indigenous people of Earth. The words of Chief Seattle, Duwamish (1780-1866) resonate through time, "Humankind has not woven the web of life. We are but one thread within it. Whatever we do to the web, we do to ourselves. All things are bound together. All things connect." It's time for us to acknowledge our state of Wasi'chu and begin the process of recovery toward a harmonious way of life.

The Purpose of Beliefs

Everything is related and connected. Nature creates through symbiotic relatedness. Air transports oxygen and carbon dioxide between the plant and animal kingdoms. Fire transforms material into formless energy and connects spirit with the physical dimension. Earth is the womb that nurtures life's continuity. And water is the vessel that carries life on infinite journeys. Everything shares relatedness and supports the whole. We are a part of Nature and beliefs are a significant part of our life. So what is the purpose of beliefs? Why do beliefs exist? How do they serve the whole?

Nature teaches us what we need to know when we are willing to look and listen to what is on display. Recall how the cycle of water reflects the cycle of life. Water receives Fire-Light from Father Sun and rises from the ocean as formless vapor. Water gathers in the sky as cloud angels singing Life's song to all below. When it is time; water returns to material form as rain and snow on mountain tops and begins another journey to the ocean. The flow of water is Life's intent moving onward. A diversity of forms create riverbanks that guide the flow of water as Life travels downstream. Beavers build dams, people build dykes and levees. Water is guided by land on it's journey to the sea. In a similar way, intent is guided by beliefs as events in our world unfold. Our beliefs shape the course that our intent will follow like sand, gravel and rocks guide water's passage. Land and water share the same relationship as beliefs and intent. Beliefs exist to guide intent and the cycle of life.

Sometimes the flow of water is greater than what riverbanks can handle. Water rises over the banks and levees break causing flooding and great change. A new course for the river emerges and new riverbanks form. Floods are like change movements in human consciousness. Abolition of slavery, women suffrage, civil rights and environmental movements are examples of Life's intent rising to overflow beliefs in collective human consciousness. The floods break through old beliefs and create a new course for Life to follow.

The fundamental purpose of beliefs is to guide the flow of intent so that Life is sustained. That is why beliefs exist. Beliefs guide intent like riverbanks direct the flow of water. Intent doesn't judge. Intent simply flows like water along the path of least resistance defined by beliefs. Beliefs can support a healthy sustainable flow or they can create stagnant backwaters that suffocate Life. Our lack of awareness prevents us from seeing how our beliefs influence the flow of Life. We unintentionally build levees in our mind that directs our intent in harmful ways. We restrict the flow of sacred energy and as a result addictions, disease and destruction emerge. Taku Wakan Skan Skan, sacred energy in perpetual motion is blocked by our beliefs and trauma to Life results.

A person using substances for relief from emotional pain believes using drugs or alcohol is a good thing to do. They don't knowingly use their substance of choice wanting to do harm. Their beliefs are guiding their intent for immediate gratification. Dependency grows with every use and with the experience of temporary relief, their beliefs get reinforced. At the same time, relationships are strained as substance use increases. Events transpire and chaos grows like water rising to the top of a dam. Often an addict or alcoholic does not examine beliefs until after the levees break; destroying what is precious and dear. Life's intent moves everything forward whether we align with the flow or not. We can resist change by building beliefs that oppose our call to awaken. Or we can let go and allow the light of possibility to touch us; igniting our desire for change.

Each individual has the power to choose what they believe. And each belief adds support and guidance to the universal flow of intent. Great change in our world occurs when our collective intent aligns with the entire flow of Life. Our society continues to agree with ideas that go against the course of Nature. This is being displayed by the condition of our planet and the lack of social justice. The good news is that in the grand scheme of things, universal intent flows toward supporting the greater good. Agreement with slavery, inequality and environmental devastation is decreasing. Movements for change are growing as people awaken and learn to hear the call to serve something grander than themselves. Martin Luther King Jr. captured this well when he said, "The arc of the moral universe is long, but it bends toward justice." Universal intent is moral intent. It flows in our personal lives and drives Life. When we do not align with universal intent and believe in lies, our levees strain against universal morality and will eventually break. Our beliefs will collapse and new beliefs will emerge. Life flows on seeking balance and harmony.

The Power of Agreement

Universal intent aligns with fundamental principles. As the universe unfolds we see a constant transition of formless to form followed by a return to formlessness. This is the cycle of Life. From this observation we see that all forms are in transition. Every structure decays with time; Houses and pyramids decay, mountains erode, plant and animal matter decompose as form transitions into formlessness. Beliefs are forms in our mind and obey this same law. For beliefs to remain they must be shared and maintained. Beliefs require constant maintenance just like our homes and structures. Without our care they will decay and fade into formlessness. We create and sustain beliefs using agreements.

Agreements are the construction equipment we use to build and maintain belief systems. They are the bulldozers and backhoes used to create levees and dykes in our mind. We use agreements to create beliefs and keep them strong. With agreements we build the riverbanks that guide our intent. We pour magic tea with agreement. We align our intent and invest our faith when we agree. Thus the root of personal power is the act of agreement. Mastering the power of agreement is mastering how you use your personal power.

Some agreements support us while others weaken us. Don Miguel Ruiz created four agreements to help us break free of agreements that do not nurture our divine light.[17] His agreements help us learn how to poor our magic tea with wisdom, elegance and grace. Living the four agreements is the foundation of my recovery journey. The four agreements are; Be Impeccable with Your Word, Don't Take Anything Personally, Don't Make Assumptions and Always Do Your Best. Living these agreements teaches you how to grab the keys away from the warden and assign your faith to ideas that nurture and support your health and wellbeing.

For years don Miguel Ruiz attempted to teach a fifth agreement to his apprentices without success. People as a whole were not ready, the rise in universal intent had not reached the top of the riverbank. Then his son don Jose Ruiz succeeded with groups he was teaching. This was a sign to present the fifth agreement to the world and help humanity break our limiting agreements and release us from our dysfunctional beliefs. The fifth agreement is; Be Skeptical But Learn To Listen.[18] This agreement asks us to limit our investment of faith in beliefs and develop awareness. Being skeptical means you question what you are being asked to believe. The fifth agreement helps you live in inquiry and increases your awareness. This lights your path to authenticity.

The five agreements taught by the Ruiz family provide guidance for applying the Eagle Condor Principles. As you practice being impeccable with your word, awareness lights your path and helps you tend your fire. Choosing not to take things personally allows us to become present and step out of drama's cycle. By not making assumptions we stay out of drama and learn to ask questions. This improves our listening. We respect and honor the sacred Fire-Light we carry when we always do our best. All five agreements help our mind align with our heart and opens our sky for eagle and condor to fly.

Our agreements are what keep our belief system intact. The agreement about slavery is fading as fewer and fewer people invest their faith in such ideas. Many dysfunctional agreements are fading as our consciousness rises with the flow of universal moral intent. The idea that we are all connected is being agreed with more each day. Believing that everything is related requires much more agreement. When such agreements mature, the world will shift dramatically.

I have yet to meet a human who doesn't say they want a world that is environmentally sustainable, socially just and spiritually fulfilling. Every person I have met wants the same thing and yet our world is spiritually unfulfilling, socially unjust and in environmental decay. This demonstrates the power of agreement. We can't agree to act together toward bringing forth a harmonious world because people are agreeing to ideas that are disharmonious and go against the laws of Nature. However, universal intent is rising and approaching the top of the dam. Everyone feels the desire for harmony. Eventually dysfunctional beliefs will break. But why wait? The sooner we create agreements that align with the natural flow of Life, the sooner the world we want will manifest and less destruction will occur. It's time for us to become stewards of a harmonious human dream.

Keys to Freedom

Each of us is a Child of Earth. We have a special window in our cell to the magical world of possibility. The window allows our Light to commune with the Light between the stars. It is the very same Light that is shared by all Life. Light in your heart connects you to everything. Your heart has great hearing. It feels the resonance of universal intent. Your heart is much better at listening than your mind. Remember this as you develop healthy skepticism and learn to listen to the heartbeat of Life.

We each have a warden in our mind created by us during domestication. Our warden uses our knowledge to control our Fire-Light. As long as the warden has the keys we will believe whatever the warden says. The keys are our power. Allowing the warden to have the keys is us giving our power away to a controlling false identity. We end up reacting to life and creating suffering. The warden's only desire is to remain in control. Give the real you a chance and take the keys from the warden and walk out of your prison of beliefs.

Living in inquiry is living in a state of wonder. Questioning ourselves is not questioning our true essence. We are merely doubting the knowledge we carry. Our knowledge is only symbols accumulating in our mind. We are the ones who give our knowledge power and Life. Being in inquiry is being skeptical of what we think is true. It isn't personal. We don't assume to know when we do not know. We simply wonder and ponder possibilities. Learning to question ourselves helps us to develop awareness and reclaim personal power. Who is investing your faith into ideas and creating your beliefs? Is it your true divine essence or the warden of your mind? Who is making agreements and maintaining your belief system? Is your intent being guided by false beliefs and agreements or are you awake and stewarding the flow of your life-force. Who has your keys? Who controls your power; your Fire-Light?

Words carry intent. Through shared meaning and usage, we form agreements that direct the flow of our intent. The word "belief" has gone through a transformation over generations. There is a deep rich meaning to belief that has been lost to our current culture. The meaning is not found directly in modern dictionaries but can be tracked down in the root of the word believe. The first root is from old English, *belyfan* which comes from a Germanic root *ga-laubjan* with the meaning; "to care for, love, hold dear, hold in esteem" It's unfortunate that current dictionaries do not carry this as a meaning of "to believe". The spiritual aspect of believing is obvious in this original root. Holding a belief as an idea we love and hold dear carries a greater spiritual orientation than our modern definition of "something accepted as true". It's easy to accept what others love when it is different from what you love. A sample exchange may be, "Oh I see, you love that. Well, I love this." It's much harder to accept someone else's truth. Also, it's easier to let go of ideas when we don't hold them as true, but instead something lovely that we care for. Human consciousness has drifted away from sacred relatedness and the evidence is in our language.

Awareness allows us to see illusions and gives us the opportunity to choose a new course. The place where faith meets power and will is the place of rebirth and unification with universal consciousness. Looking through our magic window allows universal truth to resonate in our heart. Each of us has a window to the sacred in our cell of beliefs. The keys to freedom are our personal power. Whoever has the keys directs our intent and faith. The keys can be used to either lock us in a prison of beliefs or they can be used to free us from ideas that limit our creativity, compassion and aliveness.

You are the steward of your beliefs. Only you can observe and become aware of your disharmony. Only you can release the faith energy bound in lies you hold to be true. Only you can take the keys and unlock the cell door. Your experience, your perception and your dream is for you to steward, take care of and honor. When we become the steward of our original seed, we realize our magnificent creative potential. The keys are always there for us to use as we choose. Learning to use your keys is the path to enlightenment.

<u>Inquiry on Belief, Faith and Agreements</u>

Discovering Beliefs

Unhappiness has many forms and can be recognized through many sensations of emotions. Notice whenever you experience emotions of discontent such as anger, upset, sadness, guilt, remorse, shame, discomfort, jealousy, envy, self-pity, greed, inferiority, resentment, and any other forms you can identify. While you are experiencing the emotion or shortly after it subsides, see if you can track the idea, notion, concept or memory you hold to be true that justifies, legitimizes or gives reason for the emotion.

This is an inquiry to discover the belief you hold that allows the emotion to make sense. Create a list of your beliefs by completing this statement, "I feel this way because … "

Examining Agreements

Ponder your daily activities and take note of the times you feel a sense of unease or discontent. Ask yourself these questions and create a list:

What ideas, notions or concepts justify what I'm feeling?

What ideas do I call true?

What ideas and notions do I defend?

What agreements do I seek from others? What does their agreement provide me?

Create your list before doing the next exercise.

Exploring Faith Energy

Explore your list of beliefs and agreements. Feel the energetic charge that each carries. Are the personal ones stronger than the social ones? Notice how some are more volatile than others.

Contemplate the energy that is associated with the items on the list. See if you can get a sense of the energy that is committed to holding the idea "right" or "true". See if you can feel this "faith energy".

Look at all the list and feel all the committed energy being assigned to maintain your list of agreements and beliefs.

Imagine that energy being free and available for healing your body or doing something you love. Imagine if it were available for you to be more present to enjoy each moment.

CHAPTER SEVEN

A Creation Story

Before there were people, places and things, before there was time, before anything existed, there was vastness in total stillness. All was expansive, indefinable and limitless. All was uniform. There was no uniqueness, no individuality, everything was the same everywhere. It was like white dots on white paper or black dots on black paper. There was no way to distinguish one thing from another. Sameness was everywhere. All was still. Eternity was simply motionless infinite oneness.

In all of this was a tiny urge that slowly began to grow. Soon it became desire. Desire grew into powerful passion. Love longed for something more. Love wanted experience and was wondering, "What's next?" Love's desire was felt everywhere. Then, magic happened and out of Love was born Life. Love felt happiness because Life is the vessel of Love's experience. Love embraced Life. Together they sang, "What's next?" in beautiful harmony. And passion grew.

In an explosion of light, a wonderful miracle occurred. The infinite oneness was filled with light. In that moment everything changed. Light carried Life everywhere. Love smiled realizing that light is the messenger of Life and saw that everything contained light and was alive.

What was uniform showed variation. What was still, began moving. What was sameness displayed differences. Something amazing was happening. Everything was changing. What was motionless oneness became harmonious animated diversity. Through the light all was connected, unity remained. Out of Love came light so Life could hear Love's desire. The universe felt great joy and delight.

Love was very pleased. Communion with Life through light is wonderful. "Now that we're connected," Love pondered, "how can Life express my desire?" Through light the universe sang "What's next?" in magnificent harmony. And passion grew.

A spectacular dance of light began. The universe twinkled. Light reflected off everything. "How beautiful," Love thought, "everything's a mirror reflecting light." Love felt great change in Life and knew something magical was happening.

Life could taste. Life could smell. Life could hear, sense and see. And when Life looked around, it was astounded! Life saw itself in everything. Life could see similarities and differences. Life had the ability to look wherever it wanted. Life could feel Love's desire. Life had been given the power of Awareness. Love smiled knowing this.

Life also could create and destroy. Life could change matter into energy and use energy to create matter. Life ate Life and created more Life. Using Love's desire, Life could summon form out of formlessness. Life was given the power of Transformation. Love was pleased seeing this.

Life felt another power surging within. Life could move. Life could hold focus and direct energy. Life could transmit, emote and express. Life could speak and sing. Life could now express Love's desire. Life had been given the power of Intent. Love beamed realizing this.

Consciousness now existed and was in the light and a part of Life. Love felt blessed and filled with gratitude. Love began experiencing ecstasy. For out of Love was born consciousness and placed in the light, so that Life can express Love's desire. The universe experienced bliss, peace and filled with delight.

Life felt an urge and the urge grew. The urge became desire, then passion. It was Love's desire wanting expression. All life began singing. A grand chorus sang out, "What's next?" The song echoed through the universe. And passion grew.

With consciousness, Life began dreaming.

The Creation Story is a tale of the birth of Life and consciousness. Through the use of our awareness we can peer through our window of possibility and connect with the sacred consciousness in Light. Our magic window allows us to explore and see things with fresh eyes. We commune with universal consciousness when we let go of limiting beliefs and welcome the Light we share with all creation. Universal consciousness contains the same three characteristics that we have been exploring; Awareness, Transformation and Intent. Understanding these aspects of consciousness helps us recognize and connect with the consciousness shared with all lifeforms.

Everything has the ability to sense things outside of themselves. Everything in Nature exhibits a type of awareness. Bees use their senses to select a flower and gather nectar. Birds demonstrate awareness in finding food, building nests and choosing a beautiful mate. Plants feel where the sun shines and grow to reach the light. Plants also sense nutrients in the soil and grow roots to find them. Even single cell organisms can sense material outside their cell membrane. White blood cells find intruders and fight infection. Life displays awareness everywhere.

Plants take sunlight, water and nutrients and transforms them into roots, stems and leaves. As plants grow they show us their power of transformation. Animals eat plants, insects and other animals. They transform what's eaten into energy and use it for motion and growth of new cells in their body. Everywhere in Nature we see the same pattern; Life eats Life to create more

Life. Matter gets transformed into energy then energy becomes matter in a new form. All Life displays the power of transformation.

The movement we see in Life is the power of intent moving matter. Energy is focused and guided through the power of intent. Nature displays intent. Morning glories open each day with intent to attract pollinators as each blossom fulfills its intent to express Love to the universe. Fish spawn with intent to sustain the continuation of Life. Water flows with intent to follow the path of least resistance. And Fire burns with intent to transform matter into energy and Fire-Light. The power of intent moves Life on an eternal journey. We see the effects of intent every minute of every day. We feel the intent of Life with each breath and every heartbeat.

The last line of the Creation Story is, "With consciousness, Life began dreaming." Let's look through our window of possibility and image how Nature dreams. Here's a sample of consciousness dreaming in Nature —The seed lingers in the embrace of darkness. Stillness offers comfort. Seed sleeps, patiently perceiving, waiting for a calling, listening to Life's song. Warmth and moisture hug the seed and an urge appears. With the serge of an urge the seed bursts forth breaking through a shell; leaving an old home with gratitude. The seed, now a sprout, feels encouragement from Earth's nourishment. The fabric of Life sings, "What's next?" The young sprout hears the song and stretches toward light shining above.

Warm rays of light invites Sprout to grow and express Life with every fiber, every cell and every atom. Life buzzes, vibrating, asking all to join the chorus. The sprout transforms; becoming a seedling.

Nature displays the complex interwoven relatedness that is the dream of universal consciousness. Imagine you're in Yellowstone National Park. You're invisible and observing life with a desire to experience Nature's dream in action. You witness the following — The elk approach the river with thirst on their tongues. They drink the refreshing nectar with alertness, sensing and feeling for the presence of wolf. They don't linger to savor the delicious green grass that grows on the water's edge. Elk hears the song of Life being sung and follows the rhythm, leaving the tall grasses that are home to beaver, otter, birds, frogs, insects and many others. Wolf's hunger protects the grass by sending elk away. Without wolf's presence, elk could not resist the delicious green blades others call home. Elk's awareness of wolf's desire supports the growth of grass; the home of many. This is Nature's consciousness in action; the dream of Nature guiding intent to maintain balance and harmony.

Vast interdependent relationships support the whole. Cascading change occurs when symbiotic relationships are broken. Wildlife along rivers in Yellowstone National Park was reduced by elk's overgrazing when wolves were not present in the park. The reintroduction of wolves to the area changed the Life of rivers. Elk's awareness of wolf kept them away from tasty grass that grew on the waters edge. The grass is home for a vast diversity of smaller life. In Nature, awareness and interwoven collaboration work to serve a greater good; the continuity of Life's diversity. The immense web of Life uses intelligence for continuance. The web contains millions of complex connections, interwoven through a network of diverse living organisms. All Life works like a colossal brain with neurons firing sending signals and maintaining communion on a grand scale. The dream of Nature has a purpose; to constantly seek balance that tends and cares for the sustainability of Life.

Imagine our window to possibility has a remote control switch that allows us to watch other dreams created by consciousness. Let's change channels and tune into some of humanity's dream. Here is a sample of human dreaming.

"What was that I heard? ... Nothing, just a dog barking," we say and return our gaze to our cell phones and familiar voices. Our world is filled with voices. Voices made of words: verbal words between people, through radio, television and music, written words in emails, newspapers, books, and billboards. Words form voices that saturate our mind. When we want to escape the voices and seek stillness, we silence the quiet with thoughts in our head. It's important to keep the voices flowing. It seems to keep everything going, after all, we must keep going. We must because it's important.

Engines roar as vehicles transport. Machines rumble making more. Music raves. Speakers speak, announcing announcements. Through consistent repetition, the noises and voices of our world become common. A sense of safe familiar sameness appears as the ordinary and predictable bring comfort. But the safety conceals disquiet lingering in shadow. We ignore such sensations and return our attention to the task at hand, survival.

Something catches our eye. "That's a pretty bird singing up in that tree," we notice then return our focus to worthy matters; the critical concerns of humanity. We strive and work hard. We focus on what counts; on what's essential. The duties we call important summon our attention. We must keep ourselves and our world going. It's very important because; it's important!

Gigantic colossal machines; rip, shred, drill and pump various types of material containing Life we call energy. Grand ships and countless trucks transport the power gold to massive facilities that buzz and hum managing the transformation of matter to electricity. Long thick black wires suspended between goliath turrets conduct vital fuel for our continued prosperity. Our lifestyle is fed Life through the transformation of matter into energy. Power is used to satiate our needs and desires.

"What a glorious view this is! This is the place to build our dream home!" we say while standing before that perfect piece of pie, a slice of undeveloped land. Wild animals flee, trees fall, water flow alters and the ground shifts as we achieve our goal. After building the home of our dreams, we enjoy the fruits of our labor. Others admire what we love. They join us as neighbors, building their dream home. We watch as our grand vista, that glorious view decays. Eventually we say, "Remember when it was so beautiful."

Others, after years of striving and working to keep things going, tire of the hustle and bustle. They seek asylum in nature, away from the busy activities of our human family. They find a retreat far from humanity's busyness. As years pass they watch the wild nature about them fade as others join them escaping the modern way of life. The wild declines as our desire to escape what we create destroys the wild that we adore.

Humanity's dream is a complex collection of billions of individual dreams. Some dreams are shared, others are not. Dreams guide and direct the flow of events in our world. This is true for all of Life's dreams.

Let's change the channel and experience Nature's dream again — Weeping in grief with love for all Life, Mother Earth sobs remembering creations that are no more. The deafening rumble of great buffalo herds is gone. The sensation was like thunder, alive in the ground. The animated sound of flourishing flocks and Life collaborating along sacred waterways is fading.

Sadness, compassion, joy and Love are ever-present. With tears in her eyes, Mother Earth smiles knowing the flow of Life is perfect, a beautiful blend of form and formlessness. All is a glorious dance where Life mixes matter with intent. All is magnificent and natural. She rejoices celebrating the emergence of new expressions of Life as transformation continues.

Universal consciousness is a masterful display of transformation. Forms become formless then reemerge as new forms. Life departs and returns following the flow of collective intent. Buffalo, antelope and wild boar depart and reappear as cattle, sheep and pigs. Wild geese, ducks and cranes become chicken and turkey or yard birds frequenting hanging feeders. Lions, tigers and jaguar become purring domesticated kitty cats. Wild grains and grasses transform into fields of corn, soybeans and wheat. Mountains become skyscrapers, sidewalks, bridges and vehicles for transportation. Nature hears us and sings with passion seeking harmony with humanity's voice. Life embraces human desires and conducts a dance with melody played through unity consciousness.

There is consistency in the dream of Nature. A purpose or function is expressed in all Life like a continuous heartbeat. Everything in Nature dreams of harmony, collaboration and balance. The dream of Nature, that is shared by everything, can be summarized by the phrase "continuity of Life". The human mind has distorted this by calling it "survival". We feel the same calling that resonates in all Life but our delusional dreaming calls it "survival". Our dreaming has twisted "sustaining Life's continuity" into "survival of the fittest". We reject collaboration and embrace competition. Our dreaming is dysfunctional and causing great harm to ourselves and others.

Dreaming is how Life uses consciousness. Nature dreams in ways that nurture and support the continuity of the whole. Nature's dream is the dream shared by healthy cells in our body. Heart and liver cells work together to pump and filter blood that serves to sustain the health of the entire body. Every healthy cell collaborates with other cells to support the health of a greater whole. At the core of every human, we feel this same calling. But our dysfunctional dream prevents us from supporting the health of all. Humanity's current dreaming promotes separation and competition rather than unity and collaboration.

Humanity's actions throughout history demonstrate a fundamental principle of consciousness. Dreams become destructive and misaligned with the dream of Nature when they are not "taken care of, watched out for and respected". Great suffering in Life occurs when our dreaming aligns with disharmony. Without our care, dreams destroy rather than nurture the continuity of Life. Therefore, dreams require stewardship. Humanity is here to be the steward of dreams. And the condition of our world displays the quality of our stewardship.

PRINCIPLE

Dreams Require Stewardship

"A human being is a part of the whole called by us "the universe," a part limited in time and space. He experiences himself, his thoughts and feelings, as something separate from the rest- a kind of optical delusion of his consciousness. This delusion is a kind of prison for us, restricting us to our desires and affections for a few persons nearest to us. Our tasks must be to free ourselves from this prison by widening our circle of understanding and compassion to embrace all living creatures and the whole of nature in its beauty."

- Albert Einstein

Einstein, one of the most revered minds of the modern era, says our consciousness creates "a kind of optical delusion" where we experience life as "something separate from the rest." Einstein's choice of the word delusion is profound. He's saying that we imagine that we're separate even though there's plenty of evidence to the contrary. We assume what we do doesn't impact others. Mountains are mined, forests cleared, waterways polluted and the powerless exploited — all for commercial gain. Levels of greenhouse gases in our atmos-

213

phere are rising. Weather is changing. We're impacting all life on Earth and we go on as if we are not a part of it. In personal lives; we seek relief from stress with alcohol, drugs and a variety of consumptive habits, then we pretend it doesn't impact others. We compete with each other seeking to gain advantage and power; pretending it is a natural way to interact. All we need do is look at the state of our world to realize the accuracy of Einstein's wise words. Humanity's dreaming truly is delusional.

Einstein accurately states that our task is to "free ourselves from this prison" by increasing awareness of our relatedness to "all living creatures and the whole of nature". For generations indigenous people have been teaching the wisdom of living in relationship to all life. The Lakota people have a wonderful phrase, *Mitakuye Oyasin* (Mee-tah-koo-yay Oy-yah-seen) it translates as "we are all related," or "all my relations." The entire meaning includes relatedness to all plants, animals, and minerals and all forces of nature (wind, rain, lightening, thunder, etc.) plus all the intricate interrelatedness in the web of existence. The phrase implies the acknowledgement that everything is affected by every action, nothing exists in isolation. This term speaks of an awareness that what I do to you, I do to myself. What I do to the earth, I do to me. It's nice to know that members of our human family seek to dream in harmony with Life. Such dreaming helps us recover from our delusion of separateness.

It's beautiful to see great thinkers such as Einstein express the spirit of Mitakuye Oyasin. We are at a time of great transition. Great scientific minds are agreeing with indigenous elders and acknowledging that everything is related and connected. Delusions within the human dream are being revealed as spiritual eyes open.

Dreaming is much more than what we do at night while sleeping. The act of dreaming includes day-dreaming, imagining, pretending, visioning and playing roles. Method acting is a form of dreaming where an actor dreams the dream of the character they are portraying. They summon their character's thoughts and emotions as they play the role. A common feature to all dreaming states is that they feel "real" in the moment. At night while sleeping, our dreams feel like they are actually happening. It is only after waking up that we realize it was only a dream.

What is dreaming?

Recall the last time you had a scary dream. Maybe you sat up in bed suddenly because you were falling and about to crash on the ground. Maybe a giant tiger was chasing you. The details are not important. Recall the sensations that you felt. Did your heart race? Were you breathing rapidly? Were you perspiring? Such physical reactions are common with intense dreams. Our body reacts and the experience seems totally "real" while in a dream state. This is the common thread that is sewn through dreaming. Trances and dreams appear "real".

We do not realize we are dreaming until we wake up and discover it was only a dream.

Many traditional cultures teach that we are dreaming all the time. They say we dream at night when our body is resting and we're also dreaming as we walk about doing daily activities. One way to connect these two states of consciousness is by recognizing a common feature that they share. When we dream we are interpreting perception. At night, as our body rests, we turn off the input from the outside world and only perceive through the mind. During daylight hours, when we are walking about, we receive input from all the senses as well. In both states we are taking what we receive and interpreting it. This is the simplest way to define dreaming. Dreaming is interpreting what we perceive. With this description, it is easier to see how other forms of life dream with us.

We dream with Life using our imagination. We use our consciousness to interpret what comes to us in the form of smells, sights, sounds, tastes, feelings and thoughts. With our mind we combine it all with knowledge and interpret it using our imagination. The result is our dream. This is the essence of all dreaming. With this description we can see that all Life is also dreaming. People receive sensations and interpret what they think and feel. Cats and dogs infer through their senses. Even single cell organisms interpret sensations and take action based on their understanding. All Life uses a form of consciousness to dream.

The Personal Dream

Life everywhere displays the three basic characteristics of consciousness; Awareness, Transformation and Intent. And Life dreams using consciousness. Single cells determine, "This is a mineral that can be absorbed. This is food and can be eaten." Animals are always interpreting sensations. We observe animals making conclusions like, "That is a loud uncomfortable sound!" or " This feels lovely." Cats can't help purring when certain pleasurable sensations appear. We witness all forms of Life interpreting their perception. Thus, everything dreams at some level using consciousness.

Our personal dream is how we use our consciousness to interpret our perception and manifest our experience. It is similar to our worldview but I prefer to use the term "personal dream" because it carries greater relational meaning. A worldview is a conception of how we see the world. Dreaming contains implications of a dream and a dreamer who creates the dream. Dreams are always changing whereas a worldview is often held as a fixed way of looking at things. Worldview feels less dynamic and less alive than a dream. However, both terms speak of our interpretation of perception.

I used to live a dream that was unfulfilling and a struggle to find success and happiness. I studied to get engineering degrees. I worked in business. I hired people. I fired people. I competed and measured my level of success against others. I strove to make it because I didn't want to be one of those who didn't make it. I judged myself and others as important if they had educational degrees or great wealth. Possessions became a way of measuring my level of success. The more I had, the more success I felt. Life was a constant drive to succeed in order to prove my worth. All the while a deep hollow emptiness lingered in me. I was dreaming a dream that was not authentic. I was asleep, unaware I was dreaming a dysfunctional dream.

Our personal dream emerges from the collaboration of our beliefs, agreements, worldviews, explanations, values, passions, intent and past experiences. Our dream is what creates our experience in every moment and guides us on our journey through life. The personal dream is the dreamer's expression of Life-force with each breath. Dreamers are unique and so are their dreams. Some people love sports, others hate sports. Some dogs love men with mustaches, other dogs attack men with mustaches. Some plants adore sun throughout the day, other plants want shade. People dream people dreams and dogs dream dog dreams. And we all dream individual dreams that shape our experience. Also, all dreams emerge through relationship with other dreams. Everything senses everything else using awareness and adjusts dreaming to sustain the continuity of Life. This is Nature's way. Dreams interact and change to perpetuate Life.

Shared Dreaming

Numerous lifeforms teach each other how to interpret what they are perceiving. Adults teach children how to understand the meaning of the sounds we create. We call it learning language. We learn how to interact and be with feelings and thoughts by our family and culture. The process of learning from each other is humanity sharing dreams. Other lifeforms also share dreams. Many animals teach their young how to live in the world. Ducklings learn from their mother how to find food and become a functioning duck. Lions learn how to be lions from other lions. Trained animals learn how to behave from human trainers. This is all shared dreaming. We learn from each other how to interpret our perception. Also, many species on Earth share symbiotic dreams. We often see different species "getting along" and supporting each other. For example a venomous sea anemone accepts a clown fish as a companion and the clown fish supports the anemone by sharing food. Plants give nectar to bees or hummingbirds and receive pollination through reciprocity. Nature is full of such symbiotic relationships.

Mammals depend on shared dreams. The young are born requiring mothering and instruction on how to sustain Life. Mice, lions and bears teach their babies the dream of their species. All the while they are learning how to interact with the other dreamers of Life. We're no different in these fundamental ways. We enter the world helpless and are shown how to dream by our family, society and Life around us.

Growing up as human for the majority consists of learning the dream of our parents and those who taught them. We pass our dream onto the next generation; over time modifications appear through the interaction of dreams.

Our personal dream is created by us by the agreements we make. We share our dreams and agree to call some dreams "real" and others "imaginary." The major criteria for such a distinction is consistency and repetition of perception. If many people share the same experience, we tend to call it "real". Those who perceive and have experiences that are not shared by others are often given a diagnosis such as schizophrenia or psychotic disorder to describe their unique dream. It's important to acknowledge that everyone's experience feels "real" to the individual whether others share it or not. Our experiences are unique to us. Our dreams are our personal dreams and "real" to us.

The way we share dreams varies from culture to culture. And how our dreams are accepted by society directly affects how we dream. A recent study of 20 people with serious psychotic disorder found that the "kind of voices" people experience is influenced by their culture. Americans described the voices as "intrusive unreal thoughts", people from South India say the voices are "providing useful guidance" and those from West Africa describe the voices as "morally good and causally powerful".[19] This shows that, how dreams are shared impacts how we personally dream. In other words, cultural dreams influence our personal dreaming.

The researchers discovered that the participants from the United States did not like the voices that they heard. To the Americans, the voices were a sign of insanity and they felt assaulted by the voices. This was a strong contrast to the participants from India and Africa where the voices were connected in some way to family or ancestors or some companion providing guidance. The researchers suggested that the causality is associated with how cultures hold the mind. They state that most Americans perceive the mind as a separate, private place. The study verifies that cultures influence how we interpret what we perceive.

Stewardship

Mountains erode from the force of wind and rain. The structures we build require maintenance. All forms fade unless we take care of them. Dreams also fade unless they are nurtured and held in high regard. The dream of humans traveling to outer space was alive and well during the 1960's after President Kennedy expressed the dream of landing someone on the moon by the end of the decade. People shared the dream and took action to make it happen. During those years dreams of people going to the moon, mars and beyond were shared by many. Since that time, the shared dream of humans exploring space has faded. The dream of civil rights for all races was also strong during those years. Such dreams have not been cared for or nurtured and as a result less intent has been guided toward the manifestation of such dreams.

Stewardship is what keeps dreams alive. The word steward comes from Old English with the derivative wer- with the meaning "to perceive, watch out for, take care of." The Latin form includes the meaning "to respect." Stewardship is a wonderful term that describes how we are with what we dream. To be a steward of a dream means we use our consciousness to guide intent so our dream emerges in physical form. All actions we take, all thoughts we create and all the emotions we generate are expressions of our stewardship. Stewardship speaks of our true nature and our place here on Earth. We are responsible for the care of what we hold dear. We watch out for all that is valuable to us. What we believe is important, we pass on from generation to generation. We are stewards of what we share in humanity's dream.

Dreams require stewardship for them to continue. In order for something to remain of value, we must maintain and nurture it. We must agree it is important. We need to invest our faith into it. If we fail to tend it and hold it as valuable, it will fade, wither and die. Dreams, like all life, require nurturing to remain alive. Thus, stewardship is required to maintain every dream. As our stewardship shifts, old dreams fade and new dreams grow. The dream of slavery around the world is fading. The dream of equality is emerging. Dreams shift as we change what we take care of and nurture. Dreams are life forms within the consciousness of the universe.

Nature's Dream and Humanity's Stewardship

Everything in Nature respects and takes care of everything else through intricate symbiotic relationships. Nature's dream can best be described as; serve the continuity of Life. And Her dream requires stewardship. Most lifeforms steward Nature's dream. Plants and animals take care and work to support the continuation of Life. Birds are stewards of bird dreams. Fish steward fish dreams. Insects are stewards of insect dreams and trees steward tree dreams. Every species stewards a dream. Part of the dream of a species is passed through generations with a physical code science calls DNA. Dreams also contain an imprint from the environment called domestication or conditioning. Darwin noticed that the dream of species changed. He called the shift he observed evolution. Adaptation is what species do to support Nature's dream of continuity of Life. Adaptation is the expression of a species stewardship of Nature's dream.

The story in the 1966 film "Born Free" demonstrates the impact of domestication on an animal's dream and stewardship.[20] In the movie, an orphaned lion cub (Elsa) is raised by humans. Elsa is loved and treated like a kitten. Her human parents try to domesticate her. However, a lion is not a house cat. A lion has strong remembrance in its DNA of being wild. When Elsa becomes an adolescent, she creates problems. Elsa's human parents are faced with a choice; send Elsa to a zoo or teach her to be wild. They chose to teach Elsa her natural dream. During the process the lion learns the stewardship of a lion's dream in Nature. A year later the humans return and Elsa remembers her human parents and shows them her cubs.

The Born Free story is a metaphor of humanity's condition. We are both Elsa and her human parents. We have been domesticating each other for generations. Our captivity is causing problems. Humans have been altering their dream and that of other species for a very long time. When we domesticate an animal, we change their dream and their stewardship. The dogs, cats, cattle, cows, sheep, pigs and poultry of today have forgotten much of their original dream. Our domesticated relatives are now stewards of dreams we dreamed into being. We stewarded the change of their dreams over many generations. Now, our domesticated relations will overgraze and over populate if not managed by us. We have forgotten how to live in harmony, balance and in communion with Nature and have stewarded the dreams of other species away from harmony as well. We modify organisms with our technology without awareness of how it relates to the web of Life. We have forgotten how to honor our intimacy with Nature and Life. The good news is; individuals are remembering our true essence and seeking freedom and harmony. We are feeling the call to nurture relatedness. We are remembering that we are here to be stewards for the continuity of Life. We are recovering our natural authentic dream. This is happening one person at a time. The drive to regain relatedness is at the root of all recovery.

Over time and after generations of domestication, humans have altered the dream of many species on this planet. As the centuries have passed, humans have abandoned stewarding Nature's dream and began stewarding an unsustainable human dream of control, competition, consumption and dependency. Many species are adapting to our ways as Nature continues to seek harmony through collaboration. Some species go extinct while others adjust and learn to live with human activity. Our stewardship is altering the way insects interact with plants; how birds nest and migrate; how fish swim to reproduce and how plants pollinate. The list is endless. Our stewardship impacts the dream of all Life on Earth. We are connected in infinite ways. And as Einstein reminded us, we experience ourselves as "something separate - a kind of optical delusion". We are stewarding a dream that is disharmonious with Nature. And our dream is an optical delusion.

Nature's dream does contain some disharmony. After all, we are a part of Nature and we are not the only dysfunctional dreamers. Nature creates anomalies. Mutations, tumors and cancers are also part of Nature's dream. Such creations provide a contrast that allows Life to adjust by embracing or rejecting new possibilities. Anomalies are Nature's guideposts helping Life recognize what aligns with sustainability and what is untenable. They are like "Do-Not-Enter" signs along Life's highway. Dysfunctional anomalies of Nature help us recognize the features of humanity's dream that are disharmonious.

Cancer's Dysfunctional Dream

Cancer cells also dream. They are alive and thus dream. Cancer cells dream a different dream than healthy cells and exploring their differences shines light on humanity's dreaming. Cancer Research, UK describes features of healthy and cancerous cells that are insightful.[21] Healthy cells reproduce only when needed. They know when enough is enough. Contrast this to cancer cells that don't stop growing and reproducing; creating tumors. Healthy cells communicate with each other. They accept signals from other cells and work together to sustain the body. Healthy cells repair themselves if they are damaged. When a healthy cell receives the message that it's too old or too damaged it "self-destructs". Science calls this process apoptosis. We could say that healthy cells don't resist change. They sense their time has come and depart for the good of the whole.

Cancer cells don't listen to the other cells and cannot repair themselves. Cancer cells ignore the signals from other cells to transform. They resist change. Also, cancer cells don't stick together, they separate and detach from their neighbors. And finally the feature that ties all the dreams together is; healthy cells specialize. Healthy cells mature and perform their organ function that supports the body. Healthy cells dream a dream that is in harmony with Nature's dream. Cancer cells don't mature. They never realize their healthy supportive purpose. Cancer cells never learn their original function that supports the wellness of the whole.

The similarities between the way humans dream and the way cancer dreams is revealing. Humanity's population continues to grow. We consistently demonstrate that we don't know when enough is enough. Humanity's presence grows and grows like a tumor on our body, Earth. Healthy cells listen to each other but humanity can't commune with itself let alone listen to what the other cells (lifeforms) have to say. Nature sends messages in the form of historic storms, melting ice sheets, species extinctions and growing global unrest. Yet, we ignore the signals to repair and heal. Humanity's dream promotes separation and isolation within ourselves, between each other and all Life on our beautiful body Earth.

The final feature of healthy cells addresses the root cause of humanity's dysfunction. Just like cancer cells, we do not mature and perform our function that supports the wellness of the body. I often ask people to imagine Earth as a living body with humanity as one of the organs. Then I ask, "What is humanity's function that supports the wellness of Earth?" People become dumbfounded, confused and find this question difficult to answer. The fact that an answer does not flow off our tongues like common sense demonstrates the dysfunction in the human dream. If we were like healthy cells, everyone would know our fundamental purpose is the same as every cell in our body. We're here to nurture, support and sustain Life on planet Earth. Our current dream hinders our maturity preventing us from becoming valuable contributors to the continuity of Life. This is why the Kogi, a Pre-Columbian culture of Sierra Nevada de Santa Marta in Colombia, call us "*The Younger Brother*" because we haven't grown up. We don't know how to live in harmony with our Mother.[22] The dream of the modern world is more like a cancerous condition than a healthy way of living. The cure is for us to wake up from our dysfunctional trance and use consciousness to dream Nature's dream.

In his book, "A New Earth", Eckhart Tolle teaches that we have two purposes; an inner purpose and an outer purpose. Our inner purpose is our primary purpose and it is to awaken and transcend the egoic sense of self and be present in the current moment. Our outer purpose is to express our inner purpose (presence) with actions in the physical world. Realizing our inner and outer purpose is a dreamer awakening from a dysfunctional (egoic) dream and choosing to create a dream that is in harmony with Nature's dream. This is the same process as a healthy cell maturing and performing its function to support the continuity of Life.

Our primary purpose is the same as all healthy organisms, to support the continuity of Life. We experience health and vitality when the expressions of our aliveness align with sustaining all Life. And our dream is what guides our expressions. Thus, it is our dreaming that is misaligned when we create disharmony and destruction. This is true for both individual personal dreaming and the shared collective dreaming of humanity. Recovery work is the quest to awaken us from our unconscious dreaming so we can become stewards of a healthy sustainable dream.

The Dreamer Awakens

During the night while asleep we dream. Some dreams are
pleasant; others upsetting. Most of us do not consciously
choose the dream we want to experience while we are sleeping.
We drift deep into sleep and become an experiencing spectator.
We witness and live a dream as our body rests in bed. Our
dream controls everything. If it's a scary dream we worry; we
live in fear of what will happen next. If it's a pleasant dream we
savor each moment. In either case, vivid dreams are totally
"real" while they are happening. We become fully involved in
the dream and do not realize we are dreaming until we wake
up. The moment we wake and discover it was only a dream is
significant. It's the place between two dreams. It is the sunset of
an old night and the sunrise of a new day. We pass through the
veil between two dream worlds. One moment we are in a vivid
ethereal (sleeping) dream; the next moment we are under
covers and in a bed. We've returned to our familiar dream of
the material world.

We become aware of the dream we're experiencing the moment
we wake up and realize we are dreaming. In the morning, we
may lie in bed and reflect on some of the details or feelings of
our dream. As we do this, we are using our awareness to
remember an experience that occurred a few moments ago.
This is the essence of awakening. We become clear of a
transition in our perception. We were sleeping and dreaming a
dream, now we are lying in bed remembering the dream. Such
occurrence also happen in our everyday familiar material

dream. For example; you may find yourself reflecting on how you over-reacted to a colleague's opinion at work. Maybe you regret how you behaved because you felt anger and said things you didn't mean. For some reason you were triggered and lost control. Now you realize you were not present and actually upset about your inability to pay bills. Your reaction was not at all related to what your colleague said. You expressed anger and frustration coming from financial stress in your life. Such reflecting and recognizing that we are reacting without awareness is waking up from a dream. It is realizing we were asleep, dreaming, at the time we reacted.

Our innocent minds develop and we learn to dream from everyone as we grow up. We use our mind to the best of our ability and create our personal dream to make sense of all we experience. Parents share their dream by role modeling for children. Some children see their father beat their mother and assume that is the way men treat women. Maybe they see mom throwing plates or the nearest item and learn that is how we express anger at home. A sleeping dreamer reacts in destructive ways. Awakening occurs when we choose not to continue dysfunctional behaviors that have been shown to us and passed on for generations. Awakening happens when the authentic self realizes that how perception is being interpreted does not serve health and wellness. A dreamer awakens when the dreamer discovers their dream does not nurture and support life.

While sleeping, the dream state holds all our attention. When we wake up in the morning and notice we're in bed, we tell ourselves, "Oh! That was only a dream." In the evening as we reflect on our day, we recall our over-reaction at work and say, "Why did I do that? That wasn't like me." These moments are similar. They are times when the dreamer is wakening and observing dreams from a different perspective. As we reflect, we relive our dream but with an awareness that it isn't real, now. We're watching a replay and examining it from another perspective. This is us experiencing a shift of perception. We are becoming "lucid" or clear that we were dreaming and not "awake" when we reacted. Whenever we reflect on a experience where we "ran on autopilot", we are learning to be an awakened dreamer.

Lucid dreaming is the term used to describe the act of waking up within a sleeping (ethereal) dream. Such experiences are quite profound. During lucid dreaming we become an active participate and creator of our sleeping dream. We can do whatever we wish to imagine. We can fly, talk to animals, breathe underwater and journey to other worlds. We can connect to universal consciousness and receive guidance. We are present to the current moment within our sleeping dream and can guide and direct the dream as we desire. We can also become lucid during our material (daytime) dream. We can guide and direct our physical dream. Becoming lucid during our daytime dream means we become alert with the power to choose how we will interact with the material world. When we are lucid in our daily life, we do not react and realize later that we have acted "out of character". Lucidity in daily life is similar to lucidity during our sleep time. It allows us to become the master of our dream and choose how we will experience every moment. During our material dream we obey the principles of matter, during ethereal dreams we are free from the constraints of the physical world. In both arenas, lucidity provides freedom to create our experience in the moment.

The practice of mindfulness allows us to gain control of our attention. As we get stronger at choosing where we place our attention, we obtain power to remain lucid. Instead of being a victim of our dream, we become an active creator of our dream in the moment. We remain awake as we dream our experience of Life. For example; maybe you feel great jealousy rising as you watch your companion speaking with another. You feel imagined pain of betrayal and loss growing but something is different this time. You see you are making up a story in your mind about what you are seeing in the moment. As you breathe deeply and practice placing your attention on the flow of air that serves the continuity of Life, your imagined drama fades into the background. You feel a sense of peace as you let go of an illusion that has grabbed your attention and haunted you for years. A smile crosses your face as you acknowledge the power that you possess. You tell yourself what you've realized, " *This is what it feels like to be the creator of my dream.*" With inner peace, you join your companion in their conversation.

The experience of waking up is the sensation of insight. For a few moments we witness our consciousness transition from one dream and realign, creating a new perception, a new dream. We get a flash of insight and see things differently and from that perspective, we begin to steward our new dream. As a result our experience of Life changes. For example; the flavor of food changes after we create a new dream around smoking or nutrition. Physical sensation from our body are different when our dream regarding exercise is changed. Feelings, attitudes and thoughts all shift as the dreamer awakens; embraces their creative power and dreams a new dream. A new world is revealed to the dreamer who gazes through their magical window to the realm of possibility.

<u>What Dream Are We Stewarding?</u>

As a volunteer for the organization Pachamama Alliance, I speak with many people regarding the condition of our planet. People feel deep sadness when they learn that lions, elephants and many special creations are on the verge of extinction. People are not happy with the continued pollution of the air and water. The vast majority of people feel that our problems are too big and there's nothing anyone can do about it. Almost everyone is unhappy with the condition of the world and few are aware that they are active participants stewarding the current dream of our planet. Not long ago, Americans shared a dream of sending a human to the moon and made it a reality in less than a decade. We have demonstrated our ability to work together and manifest dreams. So given that we all share the common dream to live in a world that doesn't destroy the environment; provides everyone a fair chance and allows us to feel fulfilled; I ask, "Why haven't we manifested such a world? What's going on?"

Dreams are lifeforms in universal consciousness. They obey the same governing principles that guide all Life. A dream, like every living being, needs nourishment for sustenance. The food that nurtures dreams is intent; the force of Life. And the way dreams are fed is by stewardship. We take care of the dreams we desire and neglect the dreams of lesser value. Our stewardship is governed by what we hold dear and cherish. Remember the root of the verb to believe, *belyfan*, means to love, hold dear and cherish. The dreams we believe are good are the dreams that we steward. So the reason the state of the world is not environmentally sustainable, socially just or spiritually fulfilling is because we are stewarding dreams that manifest social inequality, ecosystem degradation and promotes the feeling that what we do makes no difference. Every word that we speak, every thought we think and every action we take is an expression of stewardship of some dream. It doesn't matter if we are asleep or lucid, our life force is stewarding a dream of some kind. As expressed in the creation story, "With consciousness, Life began dreaming." The condition of our world is the direct manifestation of our collective stewardship of dreams.

Since we are always stewarding some dream, it's important to know what dream we are stewarding. What dream are you stewarding? The world is in it's current condition because people are not aware that they are stewarding dreams that go against Nature. Billions of people are asleep dreaming a collective dream that has drifted away from Nature's dream over the course of time. Shifting the dream of the modern world requires billions of dreamers to alter the dream they are stewarding. Discovering your stewardship and choosing a dream with wisdom is a personal journey that reunites each of us with our power of creation. The writing of this book was a daily transformational experience for me and required a strong application of the principle; Dreams Require Stewardship. I learned a great deal about my personal dreaming and the dreams I share with humanity. Here is a sample of what I experienced while shifting my stewardship from my old dysfunctional dream to the dream that manifested this book.

I often must remind myself, "I choose the dream I want to steward." I use my power of awareness to recognize an old familiar dream that nurtures doubt and uncertainty. I notice that the dream from my domestication advocates giving up. It's guided by beliefs I created and contains such notions as; *No one wants to hear what I have to say. I don't have the talent to write. I have nothing to offer. I'm not good enough.* This old familiar dream of mine aligns with a common belief that is shared by many; *What I do will not make a difference.*

It is strange how even with the rational "knowledge" that such statements are not true, I feel a sense of comfort drawing me to this old dream. The comfort comes from familiarity; like being with a dear lifelong friend. I recognize the alluring temptation to accept these beliefs as true. A sense of gratitude lingers in the shadows of my mind because if I don't write this book, my beliefs will be proven correct. Then I can say, "See, it's true. I don't make a difference!" And I will feel grateful knowing "I'm right". My awareness allows me to see how this illusion works in my mind. It's a habit enticing me to feel hopeless and helpless. Such dreaming encourages lethargy, inaction and "writer's block". I realize I am at choice-point and can choose to steward the dream of my choosing. I choose to steward a different dream; a dream that supports a calling to express my authentic self. I breathe deeply. I visualize myself standing on the Pyramid of the Sun in Teotihuacan, Mexico. The sun is rising. The air is clean and fresh. I ask Life, "What does the desire to awaken within humanity want to hear? What does Love want me to express?" - Then; out of Love is born consciousness allowing me to dream - and words manifest.

Everyone carries dreams that come from humanity's collective dream. Unfortunately we have been teaching each other what to dream rather than how to dream and the art of steward-ship. Our domestication has been putting us to sleep with the lullaby of knowledge. We believe our dream is "real" unaware we are asleep, dreaming a dream. It's time to learn how to awaken and teach lucidity so we can steward original dreams of our creation that will manifest a harmonious healthy world.

Symbiotic Harmony and Dream Tracking

The life around us shows infinite collaborative relatedness. Cells connect and work together to form organs, organs collaborate to provide vital functions and collectively they create an entire body. Bodies join together to form herds, flocks, families, cultures, societies and civilizations. The gathering of collectives to form a whole expands out to the infinite universe. The whole is defined by a dreamer's dream in the moment.

The way pieces interact and contribute to the whole can be "tracked" or followed. For example; plankton in the ocean receive sunlight and nutrients from the water to create cells that make up their bodies. Tiny plankton are eaten by larger plankton such as krill. The krill are eaten by larger creations such as fish and whales. Lifeforms eat other lifeforms and create more lifeforms. All Life is connected and in service to Life's continuity. Sunlight and ocean nutrients serve the plankton, krill, fish and whales. Every cell in every organ of every lifeform serves a greater whole. The universe is a vast intricate web of interrelatedness with a common theme of Life eating Life to create more Life for the continuity of Life. All is in service to a greater whole. And the way individual elements resonate to serve the whole is what I call symbiotic harmony.

Biologists and naturalists study symbiosis to understand how species interact in the natural world. They learn about symbiotic harmony by following or tracking the relatedness an element has on other parts and the whole. In our case, the whole is humanity's dream. Dreams are lifeforms in universal consciousness and like all lifeforms, they eat Life to create more Life and seek continuity. Dreams come from the collaboration of our thoughts, beliefs, worldviews and experiences. By tracking these elements we develop an understanding of symbiotic harmony within our dream.

Let's track a few specific elements and see where they lead us. Here is a common belief in humanity's dream; *Forests, livestock and crops are important resources.* Each word in this expression is a symbol describing a relationship in our dream. A *forest* is a collection of trees and numerous lifeforms. *Livestock* is a collection of domesticated animals. The word *crops* represents living fields of corn, wheat, rice and soybeans. The word *important* expresses our value, love or devotion. And the word *resources* declares how we relate to these items. The statement says that we hold forests, livestock and crops as valuable "resources". The definition of resource is; something that can be used when needed. So this common belief states that forests, livestock and crops are important "things" to be used when needed. What does such a belief feed? Let's continue tracking.

Believing that trees, rivers, fish, cows and plants are "things" blends with other notions like; *Things are not alive. Things don't feel. Things have no awareness, no consciousness. Things are here to be used to increase my happiness.* Such ideas resonate and support other views like; *The more things I have the happier I will be. The less I have the more unhappy I will be.* When we perceive the material world as a vast collection of lifeless things, we feed larger beliefs like; *Our environment is filled with things for us to use. It's important for us to control and dominate so we can get the things we want. People are superior to other lifeforms.* From here, it's a small step to the belief that *people are resources.* Then we blend with such notions as; *It's important to control others to get what we want. Some people are superior to other people.*

These beliefs nurture other beliefs as symbiotic harmony assembles a way of perceiving the world. The collection of all these beliefs nourishes and sustains a dream that manifests discord, competition, domination, separation and apathy. Planet Earth's condition displays the effects of billions of humans believing such notions. Ecosystem devastation and warfare are the physical manifestations of humanity's stewardship of a dream containing these components. How does a dream with all these elements serve the continuity of Life? The only Life this dream serves is the continuity of the dream itself. Such a dream is an anomaly in Nature's dream.

Let's track a different dream and discover more about the symbiotic harmony of beliefs. Here is an alternative idea; *Forests, livestock and crops are important relatives.* Notice how a single word can change an entire dream. In order to accept this statement a different mindset is required. For us to believe forests, livestock and crops are relatives, we must let go of beliefs that prevent us from accepting this as truth. Changing "resources" to "relatives" produces a cascading effect of many ideas in a belief system as symbiotic harmony seeks resonance. The word "relative" aligns more with connection and collaboration than separation and competition. What sort of dream manifests when we reject the idea that *lifeforms are things to be used* and accept the notion that *lifeforms are relatives*? Let's track this alternative belief and explore it's symbiotic harmony.

Believing forests, livestock and crops are related to us feeds other ideas such as; *Livestock feel and have awareness. Plants have a form of consciousness. Our relatives are family members and are to be treated with respect.* When we perceive the material world as a vast collection of living relations, we feed larger beliefs like; *People are deeply connected to all Life. Our home is Mother Earth and we share our home with all our relations. People are unique and our diversity supports the health of all. It's natural for humans to follow the signs of Nature and support freedom for Life to flourish.* The collection of all these beliefs supports a dream that fosters harmony, collaboration, freedom, connection and empathy. The dream that emerges from these beliefs is in harmony with Nature's dream.

Dream tracking is the practice of observing our dream and discovering how elements of our dream interact to support how we experience Life. Beliefs support each other seeking harmony and have relationships similar to the symbiosis we observe in Nature. Some beliefs resonate with Nature's dream to serve the continuity of Life. Other beliefs resonate with a dream that is in tune with instability or discord with Life. Recovery work is a process of learning how to tell the difference between harmony and discord. Developing awareness allows us to change elements and create a dream that supports wellness. As we awaken, we regain our power to choose ideas that serve our health and the continuity of Life.

Dreams can be thought of as our predominant perspective or orientation that influences how we experience Life. Here is an example of how two dreamers can dream different dreams while observing the same event. Imagine you are in the woods observing nature with your friends; Dreamer1 and Dreamer2. Leaves float in fresh autumn air. It is the rutting season and before you are two strong bucks staring at each other across a shallow creek. The stags charge and clash. Elegant antlers lock. Steam rises from flared nostrils. Muscles tighten. Entangled horns rock as hooves sink deep into soil. Then a stone beneath a hoof moves. The ground gives way. One buck stumbles, the other pushes forward. Horns come free. One buck stands firm as the other runs into the woods."

You ask Dreamer1, "What did you see?"

Dreamer1 replies, "I saw two bucks competing for dominance. They fought and the strongest one prevailed. They seemed evenly matched at first. It looked like a standstill until one of them slipped and lost its footing. The stronger one drove the weaker one away. It was a classic example of survival of the fittest. The winner will now rule of the herd."

You ask Dreamer2, "And what did you see?"

Dreamer2 replies, "I saw two bucks collaborating. They asked Life to give them signs to follow. Each offered their service for the good of the whole. Each did their best. They listened as they pushed forward. Everything was participating. Breeze blew and heard their hot breath. Water splashed and felt their passion. A stone expressed a sign from Life. And the ground gave way informing everything of Life's selection. Each accepted what was shown and moved on. It was a classic example of the consciousness of Nature serving the continuity of Life. I saw Nature dreaming.

One event and two perspectives create different experiences. I invite you to track the dreams of these two dreamers and see if you can identify beliefs that are in symbiotic harmony to support the manifestation of each experience.

Matter is a Mirror

"And he came to the conclusion that human perception is merely light perceiving light. He also saw that matter is a mirror — everything is a mirror that reflects light and creates images of that light — and the world of illusion, the **Dream**, *is just like smoke which doesn't allow us to see what we really are. The real us is pure love, pure light."* [23]

- Don Miguel Ruiz (The Smokey Mirror)

This quote from the story of Smokey Mirror highlights a quality of our dream that prevents us from recognizing the truth of our magnificence. Our dream is like smoke that stops us from seeing what we really are. The smoke comes from the "knowledge" we accumulate. We listen to the lullaby of knowledge and drift into a trance-like state; believing our illusions are valid. A sleeping dreamer is unaware that smoke exists and is affecting perception. We believe our perception is true. Because for us, it is true and very "real".

The story of the two bucks in the woods highlights how the material dimension reflects the dream (smoke) that affects what we perceive. Dreamer1 and Dreamer2 observed the same events in the physical world but what they perceived was different. Dreamer1 saw competition as two stags fought for dominance and control. Dreamer2 saw collaboration with many participants interacting to discover how the whole will be served. The dreamers saw the universe through the smoke of their personal dream. Each dreamer witnessed their personal dream being reflected as they watched events unfold in the woods.

The material world is a mirror that is continually reflecting our dream to us. Have you ever noticed how the same type of annoying people keep entering your life? They have different bodies but they provoke familiar reactions in you. Circumstances change but we find ourselves dealing with the same issues again and again. Matter is a mirror reflecting our dream so we can see the smoke between the mirrors. This is how the universe serves our growth. The world reflects our dream so we can discover how to clarify the smoke. The material world feeds us a reflection of our dream to help us adjust and self-correct. This is Nature dancing with us, asking our species to practice adaptation in stewardship of Nature's dream. When we are healthy we pay attention to the signs and heal our disharmony just like a healthy cell adapts to the signals from the body. Unfortunately, many of us ignore what we are being shown. We see a problem outside ourselves that needs fixing and don't recognize the guidance Nature is offering. We don't accept that we're being shown something within ourselves that requires cleaning. We press on and create more suffering as the smoke in our dream prevents us from seeing what we really are; pure love, pure light.

We're healthy when spirit and mind are in harmony with the body. Our body is a material mirror that reflects our personal dream to serve us with valuable feedback. For example, if we fall and scrape our knee, the pain we feel is a signal asking us for assistance in the healing process. Emotions serve us in much the same way. Our body reflects our dream and the reflection we feel is what we call emotion. It's as if we taste our dream using emotions. The material world provides us with events. We are the cooks who use our circumstance to create a dream and our emotions let us know how it tastes. The flavor of love is sweet and delightful. Anger and resentment are bitter and unpleasant. Our emotions are Nature's guidance helping us see how we are utilizing our consciousness. Emotions reflect the quality of our dreaming to us. They are a beautiful blessing and allow us to recognize symbiotic harmony and discord as a feeling. Emotions are guidance signals helping us awaken and self-correct our dreaming.

What If?

The first people had questions and they were free. The second people found answers and were imprisoned. The third people gained freedom through inquiry. These three sentences describe our journey. As children we are free of knowledge and full of questions. We live a life wondering, "What's next?" We find answers and place our faith in what we know. Our knowledge imprisons us in a dream of our creation. We awaken and realize the way to become free again is through inquiry. We wonder and contemplate, "What if ..."

What if we knew how every action we take impacts others? What if seeking the lowest price carries the greatest cost to humanity and life on Earth? What if it is more satisfying to serve a greater good than to serve yourself? What if it is not beautiful and good to possess more than we need? What if what we value is causing harm to ourselves and others? What if what we value is sustaining a world we do not value? What if collaboration is more effective and helpful than competition? What if sharing is more rewarding than having? What if the dream of the modern world is based on ideas that prevent us from creating the world we want?

What if everything is part of a gigantic universal consciousness with feelings, emotions and desires? What if we are connected in deeply profound ways but pretend that we are separate? What if the forests, animals and oceans are our relatives? What if it's true that what I do to others I am doing to myself? What if addicts and alcoholics are messengers telling us that our society is a social cage making substance use an attractive method of escape? What if addictions and mental illness are not personal disorders but natural outcomes manifesting from a dysfunctional society?

What if it's true that we really are divine beings with the charge to be stewards of Life? What if we have been teaching each other how to ignore the sacredness of Life? What if the sacredness of Life fades each time we deny we are sacred beings? What if heaven and hell are not places we go after death? What if we have been stewarding the creation of hell on

Earth hoping to escape what we create after death? What if we are divine beings with the power to create what we dream? What if stewarding the creation of heaven on Earth is why we are here? What if we taught each other how to dream in harmony with Life? What kind of world would manifest?

The creation story is not a mythical tale from the past. Creation is happening now; in every moment. Out of Love is born consciousness and is in the Light so that Life can express Love's desire. Each of us is a unique dreamer dreaming a dream connected through Life's universal consciousness. We are individual strands in an infinite web of Life. Learning how to listen and relate to the web of Life returns us to harmony with the cells in our body, birds, trees and all our relatives with whom we share our larger body called Earth. Imagine a world with awakened humans stewarding a dream that is in symbiotic harmony with Love.

We are stewards of what we hold to be true. The condition of our world is showing us that we are not aware of what we are stewarding. Life is asking us to awaken and create the dream we wish to steward. We can steward dreams that resonate with compassion, collaboration, relatedness, empathy, harmony and Love. We can steward dreams that sustain animosity, competition, separateness, apathy and discord. Learning how to awaken and remain lucid is the most important skill to develop. It is how the world changes. As I awaken, you awaken. As you awaken others awaken. What you feed inside shows up outside. What you feed outside shows up inside. As we change our inner dream, we change the outer dream. We are all related in infinite symbiotic harmony. We are part of a great turning. A shift in stewardship is happening and it happens one dreamer at a time.

We are divine creators in harmony with the universe. The universe does not unfold as random happenstance. We are an integral part of creation and are co-creating everything that we experience. The universe provides the material forms required for creation. We guide the intent of trillions of lifeforms with our stewardship of dreams. It's time for us to awaken and acknowledge our stewardship and take care of a dream that serves the continuity of Life. It's time to daily apply the Eagle Condor Principles and manifest a beautiful authentic dream.

Stewardship Experiential Practice

The Nature of Consciousness

We grasp the nature of consciousness by exploring the consciousness of Nature. Create a way to study an element of Nature. Walk in the woods. Sit with a plant. Examine an insect. Meditate and perceive expressions of awareness. Notice how the creation you are observing expresses awareness. Identify how transformation is exhibited. Ponder the intent that drives the creation's action. The more you study the consciousness of Nature, the more you will understand the nature of consciousness. This exercise will deepen your understanding of awareness, transformation and intent, increase your empathy and connect you to the great web of Life that is home to universal consciousness.

Identifying your values

Stewardship is taking care of, honoring and tending what is important to you. It is the expression of duty to maintain and sustain something. Stewardship is you taking care of what you value. Think of the things you value and write down what you think you value. What are you taking care of on a regular basis? What do you honor? What do you tend to regularly? Be honest with yourself and seek to find all that you hold dear and true. Record your discoveries. *It is important to complete this exercise before moving on to the next.*

Realizing your Stewardship

How can we tell what we value? Given our mind contains many influences of domestication, can we trust what we think we value? How can we identify what really matters and what is truly important to us? The way to determine what we value is by observing our actions. For example; if we claim we value honesty, then we tell "little white lies" to avoid negative consequences. Does this mean we don't value honesty? Well, sort of. The moment we lie, we value something more than honesty. Values are like that. For us to become clear of what we value it's important to examine our actions. They are a reliable source of accurate expression of values; even if we don't like what we discover.

Examine all the values you recorded in the previous exercise. Mark any items where you find you acted in violation with what you thought you value. Identify what you held of higher value at the time you acted.

Be honest with yourself. Reflect on your actions. Take note of what you do. Identify what you value by what you do. When you create some form of unhappiness, see if you can identify what you are stewarding. What are you telling yourself in order to justify your unhappy feeling?

Symbiotic Harmony and Dream Tracking

Reread the story of Dreamer1 and Dreamer2 watching the two bucks during rutting season.

Track the dream of Dreamer1. Find as many beliefs as you can identify that support what Dreamer1 describes. Ask yourself questions such as, "What must Dreamer1 believe in order to see two bucks competing for dominance? What ideas support the notion of *survival of the fittest?*" Examine each statement of Dreamer1's description. Seek to find connectedness between ideas. Identify other ideas that are in symbiotic harmony with Dreamer1's dream. Try to feel the relationships among the ideas. See if you can sense how the ideas nurture and support each other to make the dream "real" and "true" for Dreamer1.

Track the dream of Dreamer2. Repeat the process for the description given by Dreamer2. Find as many ideas that are in symbiotic harmony with Dreamer2's dream.

Notice how you are with this exercise. Do you agree more with Dreamer1 or Dreamer2? Does one feel more true or accurate than the other? Ask yourself why? What beliefs do you share? What beliefs do you disagree with? Are you willing to play with the other dream and feel what it is like? See if you can let go and dream the other dream.

Record your Dreams (Material World)

Night dreams are not the subject matter of this exercise. Our desires and aspirations are represented in our "daydreams". These are valuable to understand and help us recognize what matters to us.

Do some deep breathing and relaxation meditation. Obtain peace and tranquility.

Contemplate all your dreams, your aspirations, your desires.

Write down the things you do, have done and conceived of doing. Fill a page with past and present dreams and aspirations.

It is important to complete this exercise before moving on to the next.

Stewardship Relationship with Material World

Examine your past and present dreams. For each dream, examine the actions you are taking or not taking. Look at your stewardship of your dreams. Are you being a consistent steward? If not, ask yourself what you are being a steward of if not your dream? What dreams are you stewarding? Remember, we are always stewarding a dream. Seek to find clarity of which dreams your actions support. If you are not stewarding your personal dream, what dream are your actions sustaining?

CHAPTER EIGHT

Walking in Beauty

"A ritual becomes the match that lights the kindred celebration candle of sacred moments long ago... tantalizing these entombed spirits to surface again."

- Wes Adamson

Afternoon shadows dance over pebbles, grass and sand. Leafy shrubs giggle as they're tickled by a gentle breeze. People form a circle around stones lying on the desert mesa. They share focused intent to be the essence of ceremony. Sage smoke rises as rattles ring. Communion with the spirit of Life begins.

With arms raised the elder affirms, "Glorious Sun, your light and warmth delivers Life and sustains all we require to express the aliveness that flows through us, from you. Thank you for each fresh sunrise, every new day and all the glorious sunsets. We thank you for your light that is in us."

Looking to the sky the elder declares, "We express gratitude to Night. You carry the light between the stars and connect us to eternity. You share your wisdom and carry our prayers out to the universe. You comfort us and take the trials of our day away. You refresh us and prepare us for new beginnings. We thank you for your light that is in us."

Gracefully bending, the elder continues as fingers caress the desert sand, "We express admiration to Mother Earth, our island of Life in the vastness of space. You are the womb of Life. Your trees and mountains give us shelter. Your plants and animals provide us sustenance. You provide everything for our continued existence. You teach us how to live and share Life. We humbly thank you Mother for all you give. We cherish you and love you."

Rising with a subtle swirl the elder says, "We declare admiration to all Fires in the universe, the Fires in the stars, and the Fire in us. We thank you for your warmth. We thank you for your power. You provide the creative force that ignites inspiration. You burn what no longer serves to make room for new growth. Thank you Fire for the power of transformation. We thank you, honor you and hold you with deep respect."

A pause lingers. A breeze tickles leaves and their giggle fades. Stillness remains. With eyes closed the elder speaks, "We declare admiration to Air. You connect us to the plant kingdom. Through you, with each breath, we feed the plants

254

our love giving them what they require. With each breath we receive their love, as they give us what we need. Thank you for showing us how to follow our breath to find stillness. You carry our words allowing us to speak and bring our songs to the Holy. Thank you Air for being the vehicle for communion."

Traveling clouds smile as birdsong echoes expressed intent, "We declare admiration to Water. You are the chief of all elements. You carry Life and so much more. You vibrate, resonate and move waves of Life. You dwell deep underground and float high in the sky. You are in everything and nurture all Life. You carry Life from form to form as Life eats Life creating more Life. Thank you Water, for holding our emotions and showing us how to purify and clean ourselves."

Rattles rave as the elder completes the group's declaration of admiration, "We give thanks to creator for all creations, for all the glorious expressions of Light, Life and Love. May the aliveness and sacredness that is this place nurture the aliveness and sacredness that is us. May we have willingness, courage and strength to see with clarity compassion and understanding. May we recognize relatedness in every moment. May we express the sacredness of all things in every action."

A rainbow of colors unfold as blankets are laid on the ground. Silently everyone sits around a ring defined by stones on the desert sand. Only the elder remains standing; alone in the middle of a small circle, centered in the large medicine wheel. All attention is directed to the center.

The elder speaks, "Open your heart and mind. Listen to the stones, air and sky. The spirit of Life speaks through all that exists. Allow yourself to listen. Life is with us in this medicine wheel. This wheel represents wisdom that resides in the light that is you. Join with these teachings and allow yourself access to your eternal internal wisdom. How we walk the road of Life with the material world is represented here."

"Today's teaching is walking in beauty through Life. Walking the beauty way is living in harmony with Life. Walking in beauty is maintaining alignment between our heart, mind and the sacredness of existence. When pure wisdom from within is expressed through us with clarity and integrity we walk the way of beauty. This does not mean there is no hardship or challenges. Life provides us lessons for growing our strength and learning perseverance. Walking in beauty is living Life as a "real" human. The way we were created by creator."

"I stand here at the center of this circle. This inner circle of stones represents our inner Light, our Life essence. I stand at the place of our original seed. This is where Life originates. From this place consciousness shines and how we guide our light from here determines how we walk in Life."

The elder looks to the north and continues, "The north represents winter for us. North is our night as Nature sleeps. The night is not black or empty. It's filled with starlight, holy -light; the light of sacredness. We are that same light. North is the home of ancestors and the house of sacred meaning. Here is where we commune and receive great understanding."

The elder continues while making a refined quarter turn, "This section between north and east represents the Spiritual aspect of our existence. Between night and sunrise our light clearly connects to the universal light between the stars. Our purity is bright and perfect. The journey from night to day is like the moment of conception when we depart the spirit plane and begin our adventure in human form. The east represents new beginnings, spring and Air. East symbolizes sacred communion; a fresh new dawn."

The elder's cane marks a large "S" in the sand labeling one quarter of the circle "Spiritual". Rotating toward the south, the elder resumes, "This section between east and south represents the Physical aspects of our existence. This is where we join our sacredness with physical expression. Our body is our temple and the first entrance into form from sacred formlessness. As we leave night and pass through dawn, we begin our day by reuniting with our body and the material world. The south represents summer and Earth. South symbolizes sacred collaboration with the day's material world."

A large "P" is written in the sand labeling this quarter of the circle "Physical". Turning to the west, the elder says, "The slice between south and west represents the Emotional aspects of existence. This is where we feel the sacredness of Life through the physical dimension. We feel all the emotions that we create; sadness, grief, gratitude, joy and love are but a few of the feelings available to us. Through our feelings we offer the universe the experience of our existence. The Holy feel through us. Emotions are how we play in the language of feeling. The west represents thankfulness, fall, harvest and Water. West symbolizes sacred feelings and offerings for the many blessings received. Blood is Water and our heart pumps blood. Our heart beats to the rhythm of Life. That is why our heart is the source of pure authentic emotions. It's important to remember this as we enter the final part of wheel."

The elder sketches a large "E" in the section of the circle between south and west assigning it the meaning "Emotional". The elder continues while rotating toward the north, "The final piece between west and north represents the Mental aspects of existence. With sacred presence rich in feeling we begin thinking. Thoughts and images arrive in our mind that are related to the emotions we are feeling. Thoughts are how we sing in the language of symbols. A mind in service of a heart aligned spiritually and physically will serve Life in a beautiful way."

The Elder writes a large "M" signifying the final quadrant represents the "Mental" aspects of existence. "Gaze onto the first piece of the wheel representing the Spiritual. Close your eyes as I lead you on a walk in beauty. Imagine awakening to a new day with pure presence unifying you with the Holy. You and the sacredness of Life are one. With awareness and total stillness you experience yourself joining your body and experiencing all the sensations that are present. Your presence saturates your body; your personal temple of holiness; your vehicle for sacred expression. Desire for emotion emerges. You choose to offer love to the universe. You feel gratitude for beautiful sensations. Thoughts arrive and you see how you will express your aliveness this day."

Silence flickers as a breeze tickles more leaves. The elder continues, "The beauty way can only be achieved by guiding our Life-force energy around the wheel in this direction. If you begin at the center from source, move to the north then turn west, you guide your consciousness to the mind first. This produces a different Life experience."

The Elder turns counterclockwise from north to west while describing how the experience of Life unfolds, "The mind does not always align with the sacred. The mind can accept ideas and notions that are totally unrelated to the continuity of Life and the Holy. Then emotions arrive as the mind dwells on mental matters. Rage, anger and mind based fear appear. Our body shouts and expresses the discord flowing through the mind. Often the sacred and holy are not present in any thought or emotion. Such is the way of Life without beauty."

The Elder gazes deep into eyes while speaking, "Real humans swim, bathe and bask in the holiness and sacredness of Life. Real humans honor relationship with the holy. Real humans listen to Life and live spiritually. Are you real or something else? Only you know your truth."

"Each day is a new day. Each breath is a new beginning and every moment is a new dawn. You are free to choose how you will walk in Life. You can choose to walk in beauty or walk a different path. The choice is yours alone. No one chooses your path for you."

"May the words you have heard be seeds that sprout, grow and bloom; allowing you to walk in beauty."

Secrets of Ritual

"Humans are amazing ritual animals, and it must be understood that the Tzutujil, nor any other real intact people, do not 'practice' rituals. Just as a bear must turn over stumps searching for beetles, real humans can only live life spiritually. Birth itself was a ritual: there was not a ritual for birth, or a ritual for death, or a ritual for marriage, for death was a ritual, life a ritual, cooking a ritual, and eating were all rituals with ceremonial guidelines, all of which fed life. Sleeping was a ritual, lovemaking was a ritual, sowing, cultivating, harvesting, storing food were rituals, even sweeping, insulting, fighting were rituals, everything human was a ritual, and to all Tzutujil, ritual was plant-oriented and based on feeding some big Holy ongoing vine-like, tree-like, preceedence that fed us it's fruit." [24]

- Martin Prechtel

Martin Prechtel emphasizes that the Tzutujil, an indigenous Mayan group who dwell in Guatemala, do not 'practice' ritual. They live in a spiritual way. To the Tzutujil, everything is ritual. Gifting offerings to the Holy and communion with the sacredness of Life is the natural expression of human existence. *Ayni*, the principle of sacred reciprocity, is lived by

261

many people of South and Central America. To the north, the Lakota acknowledge the existence of sacred energy in perpetual motion; *Taku Wakan Skan Skan,* in their daily activities. The Tzutujil and many indigenous people accept holy relatedness with Life as their truth and choose to live in a manner that reflects this truth. Prechtel summarized this thread that is sewn through original indigenous cultures when he wrote, "Real humans can only live life spiritually."

Human's reflect their truth in every word they speak and every action they take. Rituals are how we express our truth. Rituals are expressions of our devotion, respect and honor toward what we value and hold in the highest regard. Through ritual we tell the universe what matters to us; what's important and valuable. We feed our devotion to whatever we believe is Holy.

The modern world separates us from our divinity by claiming rituals are religious ceremonial rites performed in places of worship; or stating rituals are simply a procedure faithfully and regularly followed. Such definitions serve to separate us from the holiness and sacredness of continual existence. Living spiritually happens all the time, with each breath not just on weekends or special occasions.

A common thread woven into our industrialized culture is avoidance or denial of the sacred aspects of living. The Sacred, Holy and Pure have been distorted by notions and concepts condensed into religious dogma. The majority of humans have collapsed spiritual principles into collections of religious beliefs or chosen to reject the sacredness of existence. People confuse spirituality and religion in much the same way that people convert Nature's dream of "symbiotic collaboration" into "survival of the fittest". We misinterpret our connection to the Sacred and Holy. We teach each other that we are flawed, imperfect and impure. We separate ourselves from the divine aspects of our nature. We claim that we are not connected to the consequences of our actions. We categorize, prioritize and legitimatize to stuff our mind with beliefs. Then our busy thought-filled minds prevent us from embracing the purity of our original seed.

Many of us deny our divinity in order to justify destructive immoral acts. This is how divine beings rationalize war. However times are changing. People are awakening. Humanity is in transition. Real humans are appearing and working to end dysfunctional rituals that cause havoc and are destroying our natural world. Within our hearts and every cell of our body resides wisdom that seeks to be expressed. We call it "having a conscience ". When we are awake we feel the truth that is in our heart. We feel when we are not being true to our authentic loving self. We have a guiding mechanism that allows us to feel when we go against our divine nature. Becoming a real human involves realizing the holiness within and the Holy without with whom we dance. We learn to move to the rhythm of Life.

Atheism is Spiritual

Atheist express their devotion to not believing in a "God" or higher being. This does not mean that they are not spiritual. Their sacred divine expression is as holy as any other. This is true because holy, divinity, sacredness and purity all originate from the same original seed and that seed is Love. How we choose to express our devotion is our personal choice. Both "God" and "No God" are sacred and holy expressions as long as they flow in pure Love.

Walking in beauty has nothing to do with believing or not believing in "God" or a higher power. As the elder at the medicine wheel said, *"Real humans swim, bathe and bask in the holiness and sacredness of Life. Real humans honor relationship with the Holy. Real humans listen to Life and live spiritually. Are you real or something else? Only you know your truth."* We each choose what we define as the Holy and express devotion with our ritual acts. As long as we align in Love and act with integrity, our walk will be beautiful.

Ritual Tracking

At a basic level, a ritual is any procedure that is faithfully followed. We create rituals to help us sustain our way of living. Brushing teeth; the morning shower and meals are all rituals. So are graduations, weddings, certifications and all contractual agreements. Ritual activities are what humans do. They're a natural expression. Humans are spiritual beings performing rituals.

In the last chapter we explored dream tracking. That is where we explore and examine how we think and feel about what we perceive. Through dream tracking we see in our thinking the same drive for symbiotic harmony that permeates Life. We discover that some ideas feed other ideas to sustain our dream; our way of perceiving the world. We can also track rituals. Rituals are how we steward dreams. They are actions; expressions of devotion to our dream. By tracking our rituals we are able to find clarity about the dream we are stewarding at any given time.

When we track our rituals and ask what are we feeding with our actions, we awaken. We discover that we are honoring things that are not in harmony with Nature, Life and what Martin Prechtel calls the Holy. By tracking our rituals we find that we are sustaining unhealthy habits unconsciously. In a perverse way much of humanity "worships" corrupt, unholy ideas without knowing they are doing so. How else can we explain the great state of discord between the peoples of the Earth and the natural world?

Tracking a ritual is leading yourself through an inquiry to become aware of the interwoven connectedness of your actions. There are no right or wrong questions to ask yourself while performing an inquiry. Maintaining a willingness to see the unseen will summon appropriate questions. Here are a few things to ask when exploring the nature of your actions; *What am I aligning or agreeing with by doing this? What am I helping, sustaining or supporting by doing this? What Holy am I feeding in this moment?*

Let's track a common ritual of the modern world; making a purchase at a store. Assume you are at a clothing store determining if you will buy an item. While holding the item in your hand, you wonder, What am I aligning with if I purchase this? How did it come to be in this store? What's it made of? Where was this made? How was it made? You read the label and see it was not made locally. You realize that since the price is very low, it probably means it was made by cutting costs in many ways. You are clear that if you purchase the item you agree that low prices are more important than whatever it takes to create low prices. You understand that your purchase is an act of devotion to the forces in play that brought the item to you. What do you choose to do? This simple ritual occurs billions of times every day and it sustains the current dream of our modern world.

Tracking rituals often leads us to moral choice-points. These are uncomfortable places that are well known to those who have walked through addiction. We're placed in a moral dilemma when we become aware of how our actions are impacting ourselves and others. We're shown we are a part of the consequences of our actions. This is when we can choose to walk a different path; a path that supports health and well-being. Changing habitual patterns is all about changing rituals. People who smoke faithfully follow a procedure each time they enjoy a cigarette. Those who quit smoking discover they need to create new rituals to replace their familiar ways of smoking. People who use substance discover their ritualistic activities associated with using. Every unhealthy habit has rituals associated with it. When we desire change, we identify the habitual patterns, rituals, then create new rituals that feed wellness.

Think of rituals as the road we drive on. As we drive down a road in our sacred vehicle the road defines our path. We choose our path but if we are following a road defined by others that has been passed on for generations, it may be dysfunctional, disharmonious and causing destruction. It's time to do some roadwork. New rituals, like roads, take time and effort to construct. Be patient and develop perseverance. Many of the rituals of our modern society are not harmonious with Life. It will take the participation of many dreamers to build new roads guiding us to a beautiful, sustainable and just human civilization. As we each do our part, better roads appear. As we do our work, it becomes easier for others.

The Grandest Ritual

Remember the ancient wisdom phrase; the first people had questions and they were free, the second people found answers and were imprisoned. When we are young without knowledge we are wild and free. Then we are domesticated; imprisoned by the answers we accept as true. It is through the sacred act of blessed inquiry that we regain our freedom.

Blessed inquiry is a thread woven through the Eagle Condor Principles. Remaining in inquiry as to our state of awareness, presence and how we use our sacred energy is practicing the first three principles; Awareness Lights the Path, Presence Transcends Drama and Fire Requires Tending. Blessed inquiry allows us to become free of our prison of beliefs and grants us the ability to steward authentic original dreams of our creation.

We steward our dreams through rituals. The modern world contains many rituals that feed a distorted destructive un-holiness. The consequences are a society where addictions, mental health issues and social injustice are rising. An unconscious humanity currently stewards a dysfunctional dream. The ritual of blessed inquiry is how dreamers awaken; claim their divinity and create harmonious dreams that nurture and sustain Life. The grandest ritual of all rituals is blessed inquiry.

<u>Sacredness Supports Sustainability</u>

The elder at the medicine wheel taught us how to walk in beauty by waking up in communion with the spiritual aspect of existence; next embrace the physical and emotional, then have these guide the mental aspect of living. The beauty way tells us to use our consciousness in harmony and balance. Such a spiritual orientation aligns with acceptance, compassion, collaboration and all the emotions of love. The mind and heart are in harmony. Walking in beauty fulfills the Eagle and Condor Prophecy.

Decision making is a sacred ceremony not treated as a ritual by the modern world. Chief Oren Lyons, Faithkeeper of the Turtle Clan of the Seneca Nations of the Iroquois Confederacy, has spoken to many business leaders seeking to alter the course of the modern world. He spoke with business executives about the impact businesses are having on our sacred Mother Earth. He asked if businesses have a way to slow down and proceed with restraint like race car drivers do when an accident happens and the yellow caution flag is raised.

A CEO answered, "No. We must show a profit. If we don't show a profit; I'm fired! I'm out of a job. I have to show a profit!"

Chief Lyons asked, "To Whom?"

"To the stockholders," replied the CEO.

After a period of silence Chief Lyons asked, "Are you married?"

"Yes," answered the CEO.

"Do you have children or grandchildren?" Chief Lyons continued.

"Yes, I have two grandchildren, two boys." was the CEO's response.

Chief Lyons proceeded after another pause, "When do you cease to be a CEO and become a grandfather?"

Silence consumed the room. Not a single business leader could answer the question. They couldn't answer the question because it was a moral question and their decision making processes do not include moral inquiry.

Chief Lyons explained to the businessmen, "If you don't have a moral question in your governing process, then you don't have a process that will survive. That is the governing law."

Our governing processes are failing. The lack of morality in government and business is being displayed every day as we watch rain forests burn and air and water being polluted. The current decision making processes of the modern world lack moral inquiry. Now is the time for our world to embrace blessed inquiry and participate in a recovery movement for humanity.

The natural human is a glorious blessing for all life on our Mother Earth. We are sacred stewards with the power of ritual expression and divine communion. We have been asleep for eons and the great turning is summoning us to awaken. Rituals with awareness feed sweetness, holiness and Life. Rituals without awareness grow discord, discontent and destruction.

Living in communion with the Holy is a sacred way of living. It is walking in beauty. And as Martin Prechtel pointed out, it is what real humans do. Real humans honor, respect and acknowledge the Holy and Sacred. False or fake humans corrupt and disrespect the Holy. They deny that Life is sacred and make declarations that we are not divine. This is honoring a distortion of truth. It's maintaining a dream of separation from the sacredness of existence. The truth is, Life and humans are sacred, period. Our hearts knows this, so does our liver, lungs and all the healthy cells of our body. All Life is the Holy and we are a part of Life.

Taku Wakan Skan Skan, sacred energy in perpetual motion is fed by human ritual activity. Rituals are how humans feed the Holy. Then through sacred reciprocity, *Ayni*, the Holy feeds us fruit from our devotion. Phrases like; "We are what we eat", "What goes around comes around", "You reap what you sew" and "You attract what you put out", exist to remind us that we are spiritual beings feeding the Holy. Our actions are expressions of divine communion.

Real lasting change arrives through inquiry. As we examine our actions, we need to ask ourselves such questions as; What am I feeding? Am I offering the Holy nutrition or toxicity? Are my actions a practice of sacred reciprocity, *Ayni*, or am I weakening the Holy with toxic behavior? Blessed inquiry of all we do is what is required at this time of great change in order to heal ourselves and each other.

The secret to ritual is that there are no rituals when we are real humans. Being real is living in conscious relationship with the sacred aspects of existence. Real humans act in ways that honor Life and steward the dream of Nature. The Holy is what sustains the flow of Life and provides all that sustains us. When we are real every act is a sacred act in harmony with the Holy.

We are the Fire-Light of the universe and we each carry an original seed that is bathed in Love. Out of your source of Love is born consciousness allowing you to dream. Choose your expressions with clarity and wisdom and a healthy sustainable world will grow.

Birthing a New Age

"Whenever the white man treats the Indian as they treat each other, then we will have no more wars. We shall all be alike-- brothers of one father and one another, with one sky above us and one country around us, and one government for all."

- Chief Joseph, Nez Perce

"Always aim at complete harmony of thought and word and deed. Always aim at purifying your thoughts and everything will be well."

- Mahatma Gandhi

There are many prophecies in indigenous cultures. One of the Native American prophecies was spoken by Lee Brown at the Continental Indigenous Council in Fairbanks Alaska, 1986.[25] Various prophecies are shared by the tribes of North America. The ones shared by Lee Brown are often referred to as Hopi Prophecies. They are profound teachings that speak of a creation story and talk of our destiny. They contain critical insights concerning this current time of great transition. The prophecies describe signs to help us realize that we are being called to come together and unite so we can create a great civilization.

The prophecies say that Life moves through cycles of time or ages. First was the age of Spirit where there was no form; only Spirit. Then came the cycle of Mineral. During this cycle all the minerals of the universe were created. This cycle was followed by the age of Plant. The fossil fuels we burn come from the starlight saved by our ancestral relatives during the age of Plant. Then came the age of Animal. We are coming to the end of the Animal cycle now and entering the cycle of Human Being. The prophecies say that our highest and greatest powers will be revealed to us when we enter the cycle of Human Being.

The prophecies say that at the beginning of the animal cycle, humans were one tribe living on an island that is now under water. Great Spirit sent humans in four directions to learn how to live as animals on this Earth. Before they departed, Great Spirit said, "I give you teachings. You will call them the original teachings and when you come back together share them so you can live in peace and create a great civilization." Each tribe was given a responsibility, a guardianship of a sacred element. One tribe was given Earth to keep sacred; another Air, another Water and the other Fire. Great Spirit warned us that if any of the tribes forgot the original teachings great suffering would occur and "almost the Earth itself will die".[26]

The great turning that we are witnessing in our daily lives is the end of the animal cycle of time as foretold by Native American (Hopi) prophecies. Many are resisting change, others are accepting our awakening and supporting our transition from sacred animal to divine human being. We can accelerate the process by recognizing the beauty and value of what we know in our heart to be true. Clarity arrives when we open our spiritual eyes and see what is to be seen. It is through blessed inquiry that we recovery our original teachings and remember the sacredness of all things.

The Native American (Hopi) prophecies have been passed on for generations through oral traditions. The prophecies speak of opportunities for our human family to come together. Lee Brown expressed it this way, "It was indicated on the stone tablets that the Hopis had, that the first brothers and sisters that would come back to them would come as turtles across the land. They would be human beings, but they would come as turtles. So when the time came close the Hopis were at a special village to welcome the turtles that would come across the land and they got up in the morning and looked out at the sunrise. They looked out across the desert and they saw the Spanish Conquistadores coming, covered in armor, like turtles across the land. So this was them. So they went out to the Spanish man and they extended their hand hoping for the (sacred) handshake but into the hand, the Spanish man, dropped a trinket. And so word spread throughout North America that there was going to be a hard time, that maybe some of the brothers and sisters had forgotten the sacredness of all things and all the human beings were going to suffer for this on the earth."

The prophecies speak of the consequences of humanity not coming together and uniting as one family. If we failed to come together, Great Spirit would grab the earth and shake it. The sign of this First Shaking of the Earth as foretold in the prophecies is that people would build a black ribbon and on this black ribbon would move a bug. The First Shaking would be so violent that the bug would be shaken off the earth and fly in the air. The bug turned out to be the automobile that drives on black ribbons we call roads. The First Shaking was World War I and during that war, airplanes began to fill the sky. These are the bugs being thrown into the air as a result of the First Shaking.[27]

The prophecies speak of a Second Shaking that would come if we failed to reunite as one family. The signs were described by Lee Brown as, "There would be a cobweb built around the earth, and people would talk across this cobweb. When this talking cobweb, the telephone, was built around the earth, a sign of life would appear in the east, but it would tilt and bring death. It would come with the sun. But the sun itself would rise one day not in the east but in the west. So the elders said when you see the sun rising in the west and you see the sign of life reversed and tilted in the east, you know that the Great Death is to come upon the earth, and now the Great Spirit will grab the earth again in His hand and shake it and this shaking will be worse than the first. So the sign of life reversed and tilted, we call that the Swastika, and the rising sun in the west was the rising sun of Japan. These two symbols are carved in stone in Arizona. When the elders saw these two flags, these were the signs that the earth was to be shaken again."

Lee Brown speaks of our unsacred use of Fire when he says, "The worse misuse of the Guardianship of the Fire is called the "gourd of ashes". They said the gourd of ashes will fall from the air. It will make the people like blades of grass in the prairie fire and things will not grow for many seasons. I saw on television not too long ago that they were talking about the atomic bomb, the gourd of ashes. They said it was the best-kept secret in the history of the United States. The elders wanted to speak about it in 1920. They would have spoken of it and foretold it's coming if they could have entered into the League of Nations. The elders tried to contact President Roosevelt and ask him not to use the gourd of ashes because it would have a great effect on the earth and eventually cause even greater destruction and a Third Shaking of the Earth, the Third World War."

The North American (Hopi) prophecies carry great wisdom. The signs of the Third Shaking of the Earth are upon us and on display every day. The prophecies say that people are going to find the map or blueprint that makes us. We call that map, DNA, deoxyribonucleic acid. The prophecies say that we are going to create new animals and even old animals will come back; animals we thought had disappeared. The elders say that we are going to think new things are going to help us. And at the time they appear, it may seem like they are good ideas; but maybe the grandchildren and great grandchildren will suffer because of these discoveries.[28]

Genetically modified organism are everyday items today. Super-bugs, Super-germs and Super-weeds are appearing in our world as Nature seeks to continue Life. Microbes that have been frozen in the arctic are thawing as the permafrost melts. Scientists continue to work toward cloning a woolly mammoth. We don't know the impact such activities will have on our grandchildren and great grandchildren. The signs of the Third Shaking of the Earth are easily recognized and abundant in our present-day world.

In the prophecies it is said that Great Spirit would shake the Earth three times to help us awaken from our slumber and come together as one human family. The First Shaking of the Earth was the first world war. After that war, we could have come together and embraced our sacred teachings but we didn't. The Second Shaking of the Earth was the second world war and after that war, we could have united as one family. But we continue to promote separation, exclusivity and competition.

In Native American cultures they say, "The spirits will warn you twice, but the third time you stand alone."[29] During the First and Second Shaking of the Earth, Great Spirit stood with us but the Third Shaking we stand alone. For a long time I didn't understand why we stand alone during the last shaking. Now I realize that we stand alone because the Third Shaking is not just a war between humans. It is a war against the sacredness of Life itself. Our modern civilization is at war with the laws of Nature that sustain Life. We are at war against our own Mother; the Earth Herself.

As indigenous cultures decline, fewer humans are living in harmony with Nature. Humans are encouraged to accept the modern industrialized commercial dream as "progress" and economic development move forward. This increases discord with Nature. This moves us farther away from a sacred relationship with Life. We are becoming more apathetic and losing our ability to empathize with all creation.

The lullaby of our false knowledge continues to put many of us to sleep. We forget we carry original teachings within the cells of our body. We forget that we are made of star-light with access to all we require to live in harmony with Life. The same wisdom that is in the light between the stars is in the light between the atoms of our body. Our Mother is asking us to remember our original teachings, come together and be one family. Our Mother needs us to reunite and remember the sacredness of all things.

We are coming to the end of the cycle of animal. Will we come together and share our original teachings and create a glorious civilization? That is the charge of all who live in this amazing challenging time. This is the time of great turning; when we leave old habitual patterns that have created great suffering. Those who embrace recovery and the Eagle Condor Principles are birthing a new age. Our individual acts combine and are forming a movement. We are awakening the collective Giant one human at a time.

Blessed Inquiry Summons Original Teachings

Cancer cells do not become healthy cells because they don't mature and perform the beneficial functions defined in their original instructions. They have forgotten their original teachings. We are not cancer. Our human dream has cancer qualities; but we are not the dream. We are healthy dreamers, dreaming an unhealthy dream. Within each of us are original instructions. We carry all the wisdom we require for health and harmony. It is through blessed inquiry that we remember our original teachings. We teach each other that Life is complicated; but it is not. Your healthy cells know that we are here to nurture and sustain Life. We are here to support the continuity of Life. We simply need to honor the sacredness of the original elements.

Fire is the sacred element that is the house of transformation. Star-Fire powers everything. Starlight and Fire-Light commune with the universe through transformation. Fossil fuels are sunlight stored eons ago that provide us power by converting matter into energy. Fire is at the root of all our technology. Science is a guardian of the teachings of Fire. Our inner flame is fueled by Fire; the source of our creativity. We misuse Fire when we forget to hold Fire as sacred. War and destruction appear when we use Fire in unholy ways. Before we can enter the age of the Human Being, we need to remember the original teachings of Fire.

Air is a formless sacred messenger that is a portal of communion between the plant and animal worlds. Plants and animals share Air to live in sacred reciprocity by exchanging carbon dioxide and oxygen for mutual benefit. Air is the conduit of human vocal expression. We speak, sing and create music through our relationship with Air. The guardians of the original teachings of Air tell us to follow the breath into ourselves for spiritual advancement. Our history is filled with powerful orators who spread lies to gain power. Unrest and misery manifests when we forget the original teachings and use Air in unholy ways.

Earth is the womb of Life. Earth is the body that lifeforms serve in the same way that single cells serve our body. The guardians of the original teachings of Earth say we are all related. Everything is connected in a vast web of Life. We only take what we need and not more so that the continuity of Life is maintained. Great suffering comes to all lifeforms on our beloved planet when we fail to remember our original teachings.

Water shows us the cycle of Life. Water leaves the ocean's surface as rays of divine sunlight transform it from liquid into formless vapor. The vapor rises and gathers as clouds of angels singing Life's song. Raindrops emerge and represent the spirit of Life returning to material form. The rain falls from the sky and flows with intent to follow the path of least resistance to the sea. The flow of Life is sacred reciprocity in a cycle of Life eating Life to create more Life. Water is the vessel for it all. Water is the house of emotion. Our blood is Water and our heart pumps our blood. The heart and love are one. Love is the purest and most powerful of all emotions. The guardians of the original teachings tell us to live with compassionate understanding, take care of each other, live with hearts full of love and honor the sacredness of Life.

A Visit From the Future

One the winter solstice of 2014, I was visited by a vision of the future. I was about to enjoy my standard breakfast of granola and fruit with almond milk when an extreme craving for cinnamon consumed me. I covered everything with cinnamon and as I stirred the ingredients together a strange sensation manifested. It was like a sense of Déjà vu and time travel happening simultaneously. The bowl and cereal looked both familiar and unusual at the same time. I was remembering how things were yet it was the current moment that I was remembering. Somehow I was in the future remembering how it was during this time.

"What's going on?" I wondered. "This is very strange."

I experienced a message from our future ancestors - "In the future humans live in harmony and alignment with all lifeforms. Food is nurtured, supported, studied and stewarded in order to promote nutritional harmony in all aspects for the continuity of Life. We have mastered the wisdom of symbiotic relatedness. Common cinnamon, vanilla and all the spices have become extraordinary. They really are the Spices of Life! Corn, potatoes, celery and all vegetables are carriers of the continuity of Life. We have mastered the wisdom that we are what we eat. We eat foods that would seem like magic potions to the people of this time. Humans have shifted focus. They work toward sustaining the greater good of all Life. Harmony is abundant and the benefits are countless."

"We are grateful we learned how to let go of ways that didn't support harmony. We used to seek and find the most profitable way to synthesize or copy the flavor of a spice. We were only interested in profitable ways to make something taste like something else. We would try to make a non-spice taste like a spice. Then we shifted focus and began looking at how spices are alive and nurture aliveness in all they join or are eaten by. We studied the symbiosis of everything, the world shifted and what was important became unimportant and what was unimportant became important. Our world rolled over and we began a new journey and are now savoring the results. We now nurture and develop spices that support the continuity of Life. We eat foods that align with our life-force and promote health. Our food would seem like the nectar of Gods to you, my dear ancestor."

"Medicine is totally different in the future. Medical activities do occur and are important. People still fall; break bones and damage body parts. We only use doctors and medical professionals when we have accidents. We have changed how we interact with the world to such a degree that little medical practice is required. Our food and material relatedness sustains health and well-being for everyone. Our life styles promote continuity; resulting in long healthy lives."

It was a grand blessing to get a glimpse at a future that is beautiful and feels like our destiny to manifest. We have been walking backwards into the future for generations; always looking at the past, and trying to predict the future. We've been driving our car while staring in the rear view mirror for far to long. As a result, we keep repeating the same mistakes.

We are in the midst of a great turning. As we turn around, we let go of the past and look into a vision of the future that is free of limitations. We create a fresh original dream.

We can come together and recognize we are all one human family. We're all related. We all suffer when one suffers. We all heal when one is healed. We can recover our sacredness and unify humanity with the web of Life. We can enter into the cycle of the Human Being and gain access to our destined divine powers.

A new age is being born with new humans emerging. The time has come for you to be what you were meant to be. You are part of a grand new civilization that is arriving on this planet.

You are a chosen one.

Thank you for being here now.

"The time will soon be here when my grandchild will long for the cry of a loon, the flash of a salmon, the whisper of spruce needles, or the screech of an eagle. But he will not make friends with any of these creatures and when his heart aches with longing, he will curse me. Have I done all to keep the air fresh? Have I cared enough about the water? Have I left the eagle to soar in freedom? Have I done everything I could to earn my grandchild's fondness?"

- Chief Dan George,

Tsleil-Waututh (1899 - 1981)

Notes

CHAPTER ONE

1. Pope Francis, Encyclical Letter, Laudato Si', *On the Care For Our Common Home*, June 18, 2015 (N. 2)

2. Krishnamurti, Jiddu, Cited in numerous articles and film without specific source identified.

CHAPTER TWO

3. Pachamama Alliance, Presidio Bldg #1009, P.O. Box 29191, San Francisco, CA 94129, http://www.pachamama.org/, 2015

4. Keller, Helen, *The Story of My Life*, Doubleday Page & Company, 1924, pages 23,24

5. Mead, Shery (2014, April). *Intentional Peer Support*, retrieved from http://www.intentionalpeersupport.org/

6. Tolle, Eckhart, *The Power of Now*, Namaste Publishing, 2004, page 20

7. Tolle, Eckhart, *A New Earth*, Penguin Books, 2006, page 296-305

CHAPTER FOUR

8. Lushwala, Arkan, *The Time of the Black Jaguar*, Hernan Quinones, 2012, page 30

9. Lushwala, Arkan, *The Time of the Black Jaguar*, Hernan Quinones, 2012, page 62

10. Lushwala, Arkan, *The Time of the Black Jaguar*, Hernan Quinones, 2012, page 63

11. Nelson, Mary Carroll and Ruiz, Miguel Angel, *Beyond Fear: A Toltec Guide To Freedom and Joy*, Council Oak Books, 1997, page 162

CHAPTER FIVE

12. Mead, Shery (2014, April). *Intentional Peer Support: A Personal Retrospective*, retrieved from http://www.intentionalpeersupport.org/

13. Rankin, Lissa, *The Nocebo Effect: Negative Thoughts Can Harm Your Health*, Psychology Today, https://www.psychologytoday.com/blog/owning-pink/201308/the-nocebo-effect-negative-thoughts-can-harm-your-health, August 06, 2013

14. *Primacy of Consciousness*, Peter Russell, Lecture given at Physics of Consciousness Conference, Virginia Beach, NC, Nov 2004, DVD

15. Dickens, Charles. *A Christmas Carol*, London: Chapman and Hall, Stave 1: Marley's Ghost, 1843

CHAPTER SIX

16. Johansen, Bruce and Maestas, Robert, *Wasi'chu, The Continuing Indian Wars*, Monthly Review Press, 1980

17. Ruiz, Miguel Angel, *The Four Agreements*, Amber-Allen Publishing, Inc, 1997.

18. Ruiz, Miguel Angel, Ruiz, Jose Luis, *The Fifth Agreement*, Amber-Allen Publishing, Inc, 2010.

CHAPTER SEVEN

19. Luhrmann, Tanya M., Padmavati, R., Tharoor, Hema, Osei, Akwasi, *Hearing Voices in Different Cultures: A Social Kindling Hypothesis*, Topics in Cognitive Science, Article first published online: 8 SEP 2015, http://onlinelibrary.wiley.com/doi/10.1111/tops.12158/abstract

20. Jaffe, S., Radin, P. (Producer), & Hill, J. (Director). (1966). *Born Free* [Motion Picture]. United States: Columbia Pictures.

21. Cancer Cells Page, Cancer Research UK, Internet Website, Last Reviewed 28, October 2014, http://www.cancerresearchuk.org/about-cancer/what-is-cancer/how-cancer-starts/cancer-cells#features

22. Ereira, Alan (Director), *The Heart of The World: Elder Brother's Warning* [Documentary]. United Kingdom: British Broadcasting Corporation.

23. Ruiz, Miguel Angel, The Four Agreements, Amber-Allen Publishing, Inc, 1997, Page xvii.

CHAPTER EIGHT

24. Prechtel, Martin, *The Unlikely Peace at Cuchumaquic: The Parallel Lives of People as Plants: Keeping the Seeds Alive,* North Atlantic Books, 2012, page 160.

25. Brown, Lee, *North American Indian (Hopi) Prophecies*, Transcript of Talk Given by Lee Brown, Continental Indigenous Council, Tanana Valley Fairgrounds, Fairbanks, Alaska, 1986, http://www.welcomehome.org/rainbow/prophecy/hopi2.html

26. Ibid

27. Ibid

28. Ibid

29. Ibid

About the Author

Gordon Eagleheart has a diverse and unique background. He has years of experience in academia and extensive practical experience in behavioral health. He was a senior research engineer for many years with advanced degrees in mechanical engineering. He was a professional structural consultant and business owner who realized his true calling while visiting the darkest places of the human mind. He walked out of severe suicidality and created a new life that supports health and well -being.

Mr. Eagleheart followed a calling to discover the spiritual and energy aspects of recovery. He moved to New Mexico. There he practices with keepers of traditional knowledge. He's learned with; Toltec, Mayan, Lakota, Dine', Aztec and Inca elders.

Gordon Eagleheart blends traditional wisdom with modern thinking to summon the Eagle and Condor to fly together as one and reunite humanity's mind with the sacred.

Gordon Eagleheart is an author, artist and creator. He teaches workshops and performs ceremony while working to nurture a sustainable, socially just and spiritually fulfilling world for all life to share.

Kim,

You are a true blessing to all life at this time of great transition.

May the magic that is between the words of this book nurture your aliveness and serve to light your path on your journey to light.

Thank you for being here now!

Everything you do does make a difference.

You are awesome!

Brandon Eaglehart